Aurélienne Dauguet

# The Conman

## or

## Of loving and dying

Aurélienne Dauguet

# The conman

## or

## Of loving and dying

**MERANO-VERLAG**

Cover design, illustration: Aurélienne Dauguet

**Translation: Aurélienne Dauguet**

**Corrections: Gert Meissner**

Bibliographic information from the German National Library:

The German National Library lists this publication in the German National Bibliography; detailed bibliographical data can be found on the Internet at http://dnb.dnb.de.

Production: BoD - Books on Demand, Norderstedt


Bibliografische Information der Deutschen Nationalbibliothek:

Die Deutsche Nationalbibliothek verzeichnet diese Publikation in der Deutschen Nationalbibliografie; detaillierte bibliografische Daten sind im Internet über http://dnb.dnb.de abrufbar.


© Merano-Verlag, Kipfenberg, Germany

Herstellung: BoD - Books on Demand, Norderstedt


ISBN: 978-3-944700-29-8 (paperback)

ISBN: 978-3-944700-89-2 (e-book)

# Table of Contents

# THE CONMAN

# OR

# OF LOVING AND DYING

## PREAMBLE

The dimensions of reality shift with the aim to explore new priorities in order to reorganize themselves Everything seems possible, but it cannot be implemented here or now. Many things are no longer valid, but sometimes the new has no form yet, not even in the imagination. At the same time, this situation results in a slight confusion and an extreme openness to everything that may offer new prospects.

And so, it can be that a situation arises out of the blue that seems to resolve all doubts and uncertainties in the world in an instant. All questions are answered before they are even asked and unfulfilled yearnings are released. There are solutions to problems that didn't even exist before. Solutions that have never been thought of and sought after.

The Maya, the world of deception per se, is falling apart. It falls under the strong striving of humanity to create a new reality because the old one is not in-human. Everyone wants something different from what they have or who they are. The many wishes, projects, goals and geographical relocations long for a new beginning with more fulfillment, freedom, space and a wider horizon than the one that is currently available.

Man has discovered that he has rights and claims and that he can be happy or even should be. However, the intention is still blurred, the implementation is unclear, but the striving is all the more intense. Where shall I go from here? How and with whom? Even the dreams you don't allow yourself expand your longings outward into the world. Those which are still buried deep in the subconscious and for whom the right words have not yet been found. With their ghostly, unconscious outlines they paint their naive pictures on the walls of the metropoles, and they are dragged along by vulnerable passers-by to their most intimate privacy.

In this atmosphere it is easy to get into a fascinating situation, where wrong opportunities creep into our lives. Like the advertising that you don't need, the useless survey, the senseless, unwanted gift that surprises you on every corner. They are promising and blind the client. They are unable to keep their word, because they have no real content. They are based on illusion and consist of foam of foggy, addictive desires. Behind the dazzling veil of their offers of miracles hide deception and lower motives.

So you are warned. And now, hold on and stay clear about your intentions and priorities. Stay true to yourself no matter what happens. And follow your heart before being fooled. Always remember your human values and your noblest intentions.

Welcome to the „fake world" of illusion. You have the map ready and your ethical travel intentions and you will accompany me to Normandy.

This is where I go rather spontaneously. I'm in this slightly confused phase. A little disoriented but full of energy and striving. I'll be gone soon, even if am not sure of the why and what for.

## A SPONTANEOUS DECISION

My motives. The trip. The arrival. My father's condition.

I have a strong need to interact with a spiritual person. In exuberance I call Pierre-François. Immediately and without hesitation he replies that I can come any time since he is now retired. When I ask him to reserve a room for me at the Bed and Breakfast in the village where I stayed the last time I visited, he reassures me that I can have my own room in his home. Everything sounds perfect.

Even if the deeper motives for my visit to Pierre-François are unclear, I have a few wishes: for example, I would like some clarification as to my path in life, more clarity in my vision and more differentiation in the diverse talents and events that life offers me. I'm actually in a major transformation phase. The transformation that was announced to me at the end of the 21 days of the Light nutrition process, and which should last a couple of years. For example, I would like to know: „Are there any preliminary steps that I could take right now?" This is the type of questions which I would like to ask him. I would also like to have one or two lessons with Pierre-François and maybe even a treatment, and maybe a trip to a place of power.

I am inventive, I always have 1000 ideas, inspirations, projects or suggestions.

Pierre-François had stammered something when I mentioned that I did not know exactly the why and what for my visit. But acoustically I didn't understand what he meant. Maybe he had an idea about the background of my decision, a new development or a new method of working which he wanted to share with me, I thought.

I have known him for the last 12 years as an author, first of all through one of his books. I contacted him and discovered more of his writings. I would argue they broadened my horizons. They have confirmed, deepened and enriched my knowledge and my work in the spiritual field. Pierre-François' practical, down-to-earth implementation of subtle methods impressed me the most. In addition, he has a wide range of knowledge which he can combine in various ways.

I visited him three years ago, but most of our contacts are in writing and on the phone, several times a year. He is always short, but highly concentrated, clear and targeted in his statements. I rarely have had the impression that we misunderstand each other. Despite a certain coolness in his way of expressing himself, compassion and kindness can always be felt. However, he always seems to keep a certain distance between himself and others and himself and events. I value and trust his professional manner and personal wisdom.

The trip is running (properly and) according to plan. The frisking and the modern „X-ray" device at the airport annoy me.

Electronic progress has just brought about a device that penetrates and bombards the entire body, together with its subtle energies, with pathogenic rays.

How can you be so naive and ignore the rays as one of the causes of physical and some mental illnesses? Just because you can't see them with your bare eyes. These frequencies are measurable scientifically and also with other methods, and above all you can feel them. In theory, manufacturers should know exactly what they are doing, don't they? Who is responsible? Who is hiding behind the big companies that make these devices? I would like clear and unambiguous answers and names instead of the usual ramblings: everything is absolutely safe and only in such small quantities anyway. Countless, unnecessary so-called „small amounts" constantly add up to a pathological overdose. „A very small amount of intelligence" is necessary to observe how radiation affects not only the health but also the quality of life of people, animals and plants. There is no need to be an „expert", nevertheless you have to have the ability to recognize connections. Above all, you need the courage to see through the lies and to point out the truth. This topic also has to do with deception, together with arbitrary misleading as well as with the convenient ignorance and also the art of suppressing. Above all, however, the whole thing is ubiquitous, because it guarantees large sales and satisfies the greed of certain people.

The fact is: I don't want to have to stand in front of the super-scanner. The employees (who spend the whole day surrounded by these rays) can take their old, handheld devices out of the drawer. A controller standing around makes a derogatory remark about my refusal. It is obvious that my behavior presses certain buttons on him.

This time I am not being tested for „explosive device traces" like the last two checks at the airport. Yes, you read it right. I had to laugh out loud! I like to mix essential oils in my bathroom, make flower essences, lubricate my body with natural oils, but I have nothing to do with explosives. Nevertheless, everyone is assumed to have a low motive. Everyone is under suspicion. Fear your neighbor like you fear yourself. Fear yourself, and above all make sure that you do not develop independent thinking. This is how to get negativity out of people instead of reminding them that they are the guardians of the earth and that solidarity and trust are essential for a healthy social life. Instead of reminding them that they are light beings in human bodies, he is to become frightened, threatened, made angry and kept small.

Actually, you are kept as small as you allow others to belittle you. In the meantime, I have found out that you can request a so-called „alternative control" at the airport. Hand control is not much better, but maybe here or there it sends an impulse, a consideration/hint to reconsider things, so that the routine is disrupted by a short break and a pause for thought.

During the flight I complete the list of topics that I would like to discuss with Pierre-François. I am very happy to talk to a spiritual person about personal issues as well as about the latest world-changing currents.

I would like to mention that I have booked the cheapest flight. But it has the disadvantage that I have to spend a whole week in

Normandy, which is unusually long for me. My visits are always short and sweet. This stay will therefore be exceptionally longer, namely an entire week. Who knows what it's good for?

On the evening of my arrival I stay in a guest house in Rouen, because there are no further connections to the village, where Pierre-François will pick me up at the train station tomorrow.

Conscientiously, and as we have agreed upon, I write a message the same evening to announce my exact arrival time. Thereupon, slight doubts arise in me: „Will he read the SMS in time?" Yes, he does, even if he never replies to it. We had once agreed that I could contact him, if I seriously needed help or fell ill. So I should trust him. Or should I rather give him a call? I think back and forth and finally suppress my fluctuations.

However, a strange mood arises in me. Should I look forward to the week? There is some uncertainty in the air. But with a spiritual person like Pierre-François, the exchange can only be enriching, I tell myself. Otherwise I can go for a walk in the nature - his house is very remote, - translate my book or borrow a few books from him, because I remember that he has a large library.

When I arrive by train, there is nobody waiting for me. It is a small village in Normandy and the train-station is outside the center. Firstly, I curb my impatience and wait. There is no bus going where Pierre-François lives.

It is very warm and sunny, which is unusual for this area. It is rather known for its overcast sky, wind, gray clouds and rain. I am dressed accordingly with a thick, warm rain-jacket and hiking shoes. I insist that I am ready for all types of weather and never have to cancel an excursion because I have not taken along suitable clothing. But that's an old cliché. With the climate change, the area has become much sunnier. It is a surprise for me in this area that I know well from my childhood: the weather is and remains very warm all week. Well, I shall have to adjust. I was expecting different temperatures. It is not so bad. However, this fact throws an interesting pattern, comparable to a spider web, on the events of the coming week. This announces the unexpected.

While waiting I think of my father who is dying. His passing away takes a long time. He has had Alzheimer's disease for years. I find it difficult to reach him telepathically during the slow physical - etheric - astral degradation. Right now, in this phase of divesting himself from the physical aspect, I am specifically trying to send him courage, strength and love. Above all, he needs security. I want him to feel hugged and provided with everything that is needed on the way to the afterlife. I talk to him and hold him gently and softly in my arms and at the same time I am strong and protective. The unobtrusive presence, the accompaniment, which allow freedom and self-determination at the same time, are appropriate here. I am there, you are not alone, everyone is around you, the ones you know in this world and the ones who will be welcoming you hereafter. The non-intrusive presence, the accompaniment that allows freedom and self-determination are always appropriate and especially now with these important steps. I do not have the impression that my father perceives my subtle presence. It makes me feel a little sad. However, I know that it is essential to continue to give him comfort and confidence.

I think of all the people I accompanied before during and after the death process: my mother in particular, the many patients and the many people who visited me briefly but so clearly when they left the earthly dimension, for example my grandmother, my old family doctor, and so on.

I am deep in my thoughts. The sun warms me in a pleasant way, time passes, but nobody appears at the station. I call Pierre-François on his landline. In fact, he only uses his mobile phone to make rare calls. That would not be favorable at all in an emergency, where I would need his help urgently. Why did he agree when I made the suggestion to text him for help in an urgent situation? He could have refused and said that he rarely uses the cell phone.

I had made it clear that I would announce my arrival as soon as I was in Rouen, the day before. „Stop with your accuracy, your reliability, your thorough explanations and reasons" whispers my inner voice. I am a bit stubborn and straightforward. We are now in the country of spontaneity, flexibility, „Oui, oui as you like". I have to adjust not only to the unusual weather, but also to the local customs.

I am now sitting on a lower wall so that I have an overview. There is no one far and wide, anyway. Images of my first visit come to my mind. At that time, Pierre-François was very masculine and dynamic. „That is clear", I thought. „He also has an influence of the element fire in his horoscope. Just like me."

When we first met, I had the strange idea that we had or would have a passionate relationship.

In reality it was obviously not the case. On the other hand, he was very professional and very focused, just like in his writings. I considered these qualities a positive asset. As a teacher he was good but very dogmatic and basically only read his notes. I like to teach with a lot of exchange and innovations. For me, teaching is like a journey of discovery, that always keeps you creative and curious and always offers highlights. I don't just want to share facts, I like to weave in examples, insights, current events and true stories. I value a lively way of teaching with a fair share of passion, not just food for the intellect.

I'm finally glad that he is picking me up.


## FIRST DAY

House and garden. The daughter. The unfortunate marriages. My own room. The landowner.

I immediately recognize his aura and that of his car. I jump straight down from the wall, pack my sweater, jacket and suitcase and meet him with my hand outstretched. He takes my hand but pulls it towards him to kiss my cheek. Last time we met, we shook hands, so that now I am a little bit astonished by his reaction. „Relax and be a little more flexible now", I tell myself quietly. I notice that I have not yet landed in France. I am still stiff, stubborn, polite and correct. I naturally have a tendency to these characteristics and I feel at home in the

German-speaking countries, where I live and where I am constantly traveling. There you need a little more time to get closer. Apparently, I have to change my mode to the French way of life as soon as possible.

On the way to his house, I explain to my host that I have been a breatharian for 18 months (See my book: „Light Nutrition – My new life as a breatharian"). I do not eat solid food but I feed on Light and drink liquids (water, tea, coffee with honey as required). We easily exchange views about small things.

When we arrive, his neighbour briefly needs his help. I wait next to the car and have a look into the garden. Everything is neglected. A noticeable greyish mood envelops me. Three years ago it was early summer, but it was raining, so I didn't notice much of the garden. Now I find that the garden is huge and borders on a forest and a meadow.

I follow Pierre-François into the house. Immediately a depressive atmosphere descends upon me. I turn around and look outside again where the sun is shining. But grief and resignation prevail in the house.

On the other hand, my host is very easy and communicative. He explains that his daughter also lives there in the back of the house. Each one for her- and himself, but there is a door in the kitchen that connects both apartments, which means that she visits him several times a day. I get an overview of his plans for the next few days and the assurance that I can stay as long as I want. He has a fixed program for himself only on one specific day. Otherwise he is retired and has a lot of time. I am grateful for his hospitality.

Shortly thereafter, his daughter Véronique emerges from the door. She tells her father about the latest home news. Among other things I hear, that she has taken in a young man who has been released from the psychiatric clinic. He shares Veronique's apartment with her two children. He is a good friend's nephew. She is very altruistic and has a lot of compassion, which is admirable. However, I imagine this living together as not entirely unproblematic. I trust Pierre-François to be in command of the situation and that he may treat the young man. I also feel a certain curiosity on her part. She wants to know what kind of woman is in the house now. She makes a pleasant impression on me, but she seems very burdened by fate.

I stand in the background and let the two talk to each other. The house is neglected inside as well as outside. The heaviness feels even denser in the house than in the garden. It depresses me all the more. I have antennae that immediately inform me about the atmosphere in the surroundings. There are layers on top of layers of everyday worries and desires (that lie on top of each other). I hear arguments and accusations, but everything is suffocated and muffled. This ability to scan moods in rooms is part of my clairvoyance, but also part of my professional background. As a nurse and as a ward nurse, I was immediately able to determine in the department how neat, how positive or how punctual the work flow was, whether an emergency had occurred, whether there was a gross delay or lack of staff, and so on.

An overwhelming density hangs in Pierre-François's house. More specifically, it feels like a depression that someone is only partially able to control. He treats himself, I suspect, because he has healing abilities and he has written several brochures on different healing methods. Coins and stamps as well as albums and special literature on the subject lie on the wooden table. The library on the other side of the living room is well organized, and many coin and stamp albums are sorted on the shelves in alphabetic order. The rest is old, neglected, sometimes even really dirty. Everyday habits that automatically repeat themselves over the years fill the large room. The objects that collect a kind of emotional patina with every movement, with every repeated action are witnesses depending on whether the person handles the object with joy, gratitude, altruistic thoughts, or takes it in his hands with frustration, selfishness and absentmindedness. Our thoughts, our feelings and actions, our whole constitution leave energetic traces which settle in the ether, in the walls, in the rooms, in the buildings and are kept there for eternity. Even if they no longer exist, the vibration in the ether persists in these places. Doesn't this knowledge make us more careful when dealing with our surroundings?

Pierre-François has lived in this house for thirty-five years, as I will find out later. Everyday life has taken place here with different partners over three decades. Particularly difficult relationships prevailed longest. This kind of persistence is foreign to me. I have always moved a lot, from one country to another, and I kept getting rid of things. Through these frequent changes, a material minimalism has installed itself in my life, as I am often driven by the urge to start all over again and again.

Pierre-François' stability is beneficial to the creativity and productivity that he has developed over the years. It has been of benefit for him in writing the numerous books and booklets and in his active work as a teacher. On the other hand, the accumulated energies of this house are evidence of the long private suffering that has shaped his various marriages.

Immediately after my arrival and our first tour around the large neglected garden he starts telling me about his unhappy marriages. The women were problematic, he says. He also shares intimate details about these women, which I don't appreciate. Even though I agree to listen to the stories about his private life, I don't feel so close to hearing personal preferences or difficulties from third parties, namely his ex-wives. It is also not the right time: I have only just arrived, and we only know one another through spiritual and esoteric work. Our relationship is purely professional, and I am amazed at the way my host is sharing his private worries with me. I have a certain respect for these women, even if I don't know them, out of personal dignity and out of female solidarity. I wouldn't appreciate it, if a former lover blabbed out about my sexual behavior.

Pierre-François has a lot to tell, because these relationships have followed each other without interruption for decades. There is much suffering in his report; however, I don't feel any emotion within him. Although he finds the right words to describe the shortcomings of his partners, he himself has little connection with his emotional experience and entirely avoids questioning himself. The thirty years of married life with two different wives were „a huge disaster", he says. He does not see his part in the way things have developed.

He has only experienced partner-happiness with his dream-wife for the past seven years. Unfortunately, Bella died of a chronic illness three years ago. „For me, she is and remains the most beautiful woman in the world!" he says several times. But Bella was his sister-in-law, which sparked a number of conflicts with his last wife. Pierre-François also talks a lot about his relationship to his mother. Obviously, he is a mother's boy and he seems to have a strong black-and-white relationship with women.

Although I am surprised that he informs me of his private situation from the outset, I take into consideration that he has been through a lot and is sometimes still suffering from grief. This is why I listen respectfully, attentively and compassionately. I am considerate of people and their statements. Again and again, everywhere and under different circumstances, I seem to have to take on the role of the therapist immediately, or at least the confidante who can be told everything. Already as a child, I took on this role with my mother. Unconsciously, of course.

However, I am puzzled to find myself in a position as a listener and even the recipient of very private details as soon as I arrive. What I lack is the transition between my position as a student or as a reader of his books –possibly as a colleague as I have considered myself up to this point – to that of a private person such as a sister or a friend. Obviously, I missed something out, because we have cultivated a friendly but distant, pure professional acquaintance until now. I laugh at myself: „Not only are you the therapist of therapists at home, but also on the go, where you are hardly known." Compassion and above all understanding give me access to my host's despair. However, his suffering is not about a loud soul pain, but rather about a long pent-up emotional repression, in which the own shadow-aspect is not included. Thirty years of marital misfortune. And then, according to his report, he finally enjoys a perfect relationship with Bella, which ends dramatically. That's why I give him all my sympathy. The report unfolds long and almost without interruption. Later the topic changes and he shows me his treasures.

Pierre-François explains that he is a passionate collector and likes visiting markets all over the area and that he even runs a stall himself. „My father was also a great collector", I mention. „Well, then you're already used to the collector's habits. That's a good thing", he seems to mumble half to me, half to himself. He shows me his different collections. At the same time, I visualize the valuable books, magazines and ethnological objects that my father had collected over the decades. He had such a huge collection that filled a long house similar to a row of three cottages. My father's collector vein went wrong at some point and he became a messy, keeping and stacking everything until the house was almost full of garbage, empty bottles, and so on.

There are some more similarities between my father and Pierre-François: apart from the highly esteemed, orderly collection, everything else is pretty dirty and neglected. What is needed every day is old and still in use despite its poor condition. Inside and outside, the house and garden are neglected, messy and dingy. A feeling of abandonment, standstill, lack of attention and sadness hover in the air. Such an environment fills me with regret, because I see the great potential that would unfold, if the place and the rooms were cleaned, grounded and cared for energetically and physically. I would give them mindfulness and appreciation until they fill up with love and vitality again. That would be a big step to start with, before the house is renovated and modernized and the garden is newly created. I imagine what could be rebuilt, repaired and maintained here to reawaken the unused potential, so that the house and the huge surrounding garden can be revived in their splendor and cheerful vitality. However, this is an idea that only comes from my impulse to make everyone and everything safe, beautiful and harmonious again, because I am a healer in my essence but definitely not from the plan to settle here and take on this monumental task. It is also very clear to me that, even if in my imagination, I enjoy the idea of the blossoming, well-tended nature that would thrive in this garden and how I would transform the interior architecture into a place of good taste, creative aesthetics, safety.

Here, on the other hand, the rooms reflect people and their inner despair. Pierre-François doesn't admit it. He even dubs them with a certain cheerfulness, which is obviously put on. He is trying to make a good impression on me.

Since the sun is shining outside, I use a short break in Pierre-François' description to go to the garden and play with the cats. It is an escape, an escape from his verbiage, but above all from the depressing energy of the house. I'm dressed too warmly, but soon the sun is gone and then the air cools down significantly.

When I come back into the house, he continues his story. After a while I interrupt him so that he shows me my „own room". It's amazingly dirty, dusty and crammed with different things that have been pushed aside. The thin mattress is covered with a sheet. I very much doubt that it is clean, but first I ask for more bed linen. My host just stands there. Thoughtful or helpless or slightly confused, I don't know exactly. „You told me on the phone that you had everything you need here. That's why I didn't bring anything with me", I finally say, in order to stimulate a reaction on his part. However, it takes a few minutes for him to come back with a sleeping bag and to eventually find a blanket.

At dinner I sit down at the table with him and sip some honey. He also talks about his personal life with many private details. As I said, I was not prepared for my stay to be a permanent one-to-one session. I can listen well, and I feel his loneliness, his grief and the need to free himself from the suffering that has accumulated over the years. I suspect he has healed others throughout his life and kept his own suffering to himself. This is what it looks like. And now he has found someone he can trust. Is that all or is there something else behind it? I only know that I am amazed, and I did not expect such a reception, but rather a student-teacher relationship, as we used to have it on my last visit.

After dinner before dark, it's time for a walk in this secluded hamlet with just a few houses. The fresh air and the movement are good for me. Our walk is brisk, but we can enjoy the mood of the twilight. He shows me many fields that belong to him, some with planning permission: „And this meadow over there is mine too. As well as this strip of land that extends to the next village". According to his report, he appears to be an important landowner.

When we get home, I announce very early that I want to withdraw. „It is better not to close the bedroom door, otherwise the cat will scratch until you wake up", he says, as I climb the wooden stairs. His bedroom is facing my „own room".

„Strange", I think to myself, and it takes me longer to fall asleep.


# SECOND DAY

The new situation. The marriages and the wonderful relationship. The troubled young man. My written list. Alice in Wonderland. The dance evening.

I sleep longer than my pranic sleep usually requires. I was tired from the trip, but also realize that I have to „digest" this situation here. Changes on my part are urgently needed here: not only in terms of the weather or how to deal with the welcome, a clear update on my role in this acquaintance seems to be due as well. But I still have no idea how I should classify this relationship now. In such situations I sleep longer in order to process and assimilate the whole thing in that state of consciousness. I realize, I'm not ready yet to grasp what is really taking place here. I cannot say exactly what is going on here.

I meditate to gain a deeper insight. In fact, I see that the point now is to discover another aspect of Pierre-François. It is therefore necessary to rethink my behavior and my perspective.

I also see that there is a surprise for me here, and it reveals something that I did not suspect. Or did I?

At the moment, however, I am slightly confused and plan to maintain my priorities, i.e. my daily exercises, my regular work in the form of radionic, my reading and my pranic nutrition as well as the cleanliness, care and cleansing of my body. I am interested in my host's private library. I will examine it and focus on reading. It is obvious that I am trying to center myself and focus on my needs.

Above all, I take care that I don't let Pierre-François' unpredictable way to get me out of my concept. His idea of demarcation seems rather vague to me. In other words, I cannot recognize a clear line in his approach to me. Am I his therapist? Am I a close friend to whom he entrusts his private life? Who am I for him? For my part, I see myself in the role of a student, a teacher and an author who likes to exchange knowledge with him and who wants to learn something from him.

When I'm ready, I go downstairs, I greet him friendly but with a certain distance. Then I make myself a coffee.

„Did you sleep well?" is his question. Before I formulate the answer, he describes the particularly good energies of the house.

„Yes, some things are very nice, especially since it is very quiet, as there is no traffic near the house", I admit.

I keep to myself, that the dirt really bothers me, and the need that I had to ventilate thoroughly before going to sleep. But okay, the night was peaceful - despite the bedroom door being open.

Pierre-François is already sitting at the table arranging his coins or stamps. He usually sits there with these activities as soon as he gets up in the morning and immediately when we return home from shopping or from an excursion. He is chained to the table and caught up in this activity as a collector of coins and stamps.

He explains to me what he has planned for this week: Tonight we will go dancing, tomorrow we will visit a friend and go for a drive to a larger city, where we will also go to a restaurant and so on.

Moreover, he would like to pay me a big compliment: I immediately have made an excellent impression on his daughter. She liked me straight away. Véronique even found that I was the right woman for him. „She is the kind of woman you need", she literally claimed. But I don't take the whole thing so seriously.

Today Pierre-François receives his son's visit for lunch. Their mutual appreciation is obvious, and they have a cheerful and lively exchange.

In the meantime, my gaze wanders out of the window and I see a rather disturbed young man who walks through the garden very nervously and with oversized steps. I assume it is M., the young schizophrenic, who lives with Véronique.

I only see him from behind, but I immediately notice that his aura is occupied by several entities. I assume that Pierre-François knows the condition of the young man and will take care of him and that he gives his daughter thorough advice. The situation seems dangerous to me. I perceive foreign energies, I am professionally trained and I was a psychiatric nurse for ten years.

Pierre-François and I spend the afternoon together. He continues to tell about his dream-woman and what they have experienced together. He also reports on the many jobs he has been practicing in his life. Indeed, he has a quick mind and appears to be able to perform very different roles and tasks. He is an interesting person, but he seems less and less reliable to me. Now he is retired anyway, and he has given up all his spiritual activities. Some people are amazed when they used to know him in a certain role and suddenly discover a completely different aspect of him. Sometimes they can hardly cope with the revelation of his new personality. „Well", I think, „it probably applies to me too. I travel to someone whom I have known from a distance for 12 years in a special context and discover a person who actually doesn't want to have anything to do with spirituality or deeper topics. It is a surprise for me because these topics are precisely the reason and the motive for my being here."

Pierre-François goes on describing the most wonderful relationship he has ever had with the partner who died three years ago. Even today, he is not sparing me with any intimate details. I try to show discreetly that I not only dislike this, but that I don't want to get involved. He has never shown Bella´s pictures to anyone. But with me he has the feeling that he wants to make an exception. I am special. In fact, she was a very beautiful woman. She used to love dancing. Her specialty was the local traditional dancing. He had not participated in a dance evening like this since her death. Tonight is probably the first time that he wants to dance again. I immediately explain to him that dancing in general and traditional circular dancing in particular is not my thing. I am happy to come along, but I will most likely not dance.

Suddenly Véronique storms into the kitchen and complains loudly and very emotionally that the young man is unbearable. He curses and insults her. There is also the fact that he is a foreigner and that language problems seem to complicate the situation. I watch Pierre-François deal with the situation that is taking place under his roof. He seems to have no idea about the potentially dangerous issue, either from a psychiatric or an energetic point of view. He handles his daughter's complaint very superficially. Frankly, his attitude seems untrustworthy to me. Either he represses the severity of the issue, he lets the angels work or he is unable to realistically classify the constellation. I ask him a few questions and conclude that the last guess is the right one. Although Pierre-François has written a lot about vampire energies, he does not seem to register anything now. He is clairvoyant and supposedly perceives all kinds of energies, but not those of the young schizophrenic who is wandering around his garden in a very tense manner. Strange. I ask Pierre-François directly what he can say about it. He evades the issue and remains smiling and practically uninvolved.

So many little things do not tally. I'm starting to feel more and more uncomfortable.

Véronique speaks to me very kindly. She would like to go out into the garden with me. We go out in the sun together. She is very trusting and tells me a lot about her difficulties. She seems to have been attracting a number of catastrophes in the last years, so her father offered her this place to live with him.

„Can he not help you energetically or make supportive recommendations?" I ask. „He writes books with all sorts of solutions and in-depth explanations of the causes of different behavior and lifestyle changes."

„No, he doesn't want to interfere", she says. „She should rather turn to me for it." I can partially understand his position. But there are simple means and possibilities that have a very stabilizing effect, which he could recommend without obligation. Our conversation is interrupted: Véronique now has to pick up her children from school.

I remain thoughtful, alone in the garden. I sit in the grass and happily play with the cats. Animals always have a balancing and beneficial effect on me. Are my concerns about the condition of the young man exaggerated, because I have experienced very acute situations during my psychiatric nursing job? He was released, because he has no health insurance in this country, not because he is healthy. It is irresponsible to send a homeless person suffering from psychotic symptoms outside into the community. It even seems potentially dangerous to me. Véronique has a good heart, but she has no idea of the scope of her decision to house him. Neither does my host, who allows a person with acute psychiatric symptoms to live under his roof and share the apartment with his daughter and her children. These are my considerations about this situation, which gradually feels more and more inconsistent.

Pierre-François looks outside. „How's Alice in Wonderland doing?" He calls from the front steps. I can hardly refrain a sarcastic smile. I'm a little too old to be compared with Alice. And I see no trace of the so-called wonderland. How wrong can he be? He is able to perceive auras. Do I just have the radiant aura of Alice in Wonderland? I actually know her well, because this is the first book that my father read to me when I was a child. It was a beautiful old book with original illustrations, which I meticulously examined with my father during the reading breaks. In fact, I see some parallels with Alice. I can slip into another reality in an instant and find myself in a completely different world, where I intuitively and energetically follow both internal and external processes. By this I mean psychological and psychic processes as well as external events that take place simultaneously. For example, I get to know what a person feels and thinks and how these feelings and thoughts influence the outside world and vice versa. Comparable to dreams, where the layers of reality flow into one another. This usually happens to me involuntarily. These processes occur without my doing so, although the resulting shifts in consciousness often provide answers to questions or relevant aspects of interest. For example, several decades ago I was initiated into the mysteries of the dying process by a car accident that happened before my eyes and that threw the deadly injured person right at my feet. And I now slip into this wasteland somewhere in Normandy with this man, who no longer wants to be a spiritual teacher and author, with his problem-laden daughter, a single mother, and the young man with schizophrenia. The whole thing in the sad, neglected house in the middle of the unkempt garden. Involuntarily, so to say. This is definitely not what I was looking for.

A little later I return to the house and make tea for Pierre-François and me. Maybe we can give the whole thing a structure or an interesting turn. I had prepared a list on the way here, a list of topics, questions, priorities that I would like to go through with him. For some we may need a teaching framework, but others we can treat more casually. I also wanted to receive treatment from him and pay a visit to a place of power, of which there are so many in the area.

He quickly goes through the list. His answers are short, rather superficial and particularly uninterested. I don't need the treatment. The energies of the house are great and soothing. They always worked on us even in our sleep. We also do each other a lot of good. „Then we let it unfold", he says with a smile.

What should I think of this answer? My fingers roll my list into a tube. I was especially happy to spend time with this valuable person. I specifically wanted to make this stay enriching. I arrived with a spiritual thirst. Here it will not be. I have to open my eyes and look at the situation properly. Not only has the weather changed, but the inspiring author is at the end of his wits. Something else is coming up. I feel confused, because I am still unable to assess the unexpected set up I find myself in. No panic.

„Am I too stubborn" I ask my inner voice. „Should I be more flexible? What exactly is going on here?"

„Take your time", she replies. „You can be as stubborn or as flexible as you want. But above all, don't let anything happen to you, but stick to your credo, stay awake. You decide what you want, when and how it should happen." I am just observing, both my own reactions and the suggestions that Pierre-François is coming up with.

My host sits with his coins for hours. I translate my last book into French. Every now and then I need exercise and go to the garden. The young man is walking there with great strides and seems to be very charged. Thank God that the park is so vast and that he has a lot of space to vent his frustration through the movement. He remains far away on the edge of the green area.

Three generations are happily thriving in the house: grandfather, daughter and the two children. They are loud and busy and finally bring joy and movement in this dark environment. I am enjoying this lightness. It doesn't last very long, because a catastrophe happens and one of the children roars so loudly that the grandfather sends the small family away to their part of the house. With relief he closes the door between the kitchen and the daughter's apartment.

After dinner, it's time to get ready for the traditional dance night.

On my part, however, there is not much to prepare, because I have not brought any suitable clothes with me. Not even lighter shoes. But it suits me perfectly. I definitely won't dance.

The evening is pleasant, the people are friendly. The former girlfriend was such a great dancer, that I don't even have to try and compete. With me the attempt remains nipped in the bud. I don't feel like it and I am not relaxed at all. But I laugh a lot with a lady who, for medical reasons, is not allowed to dance, but joins the circle whenever she is asked. But we happen to sit together time and time again. She keeps complimenting me about my „friend". He is so nice. I'm lucky that he comes to me after every dance. He is so attentive. I want to tell her right away that she can have the nice man, because he is not „my friend". But in no time, she is gone, seduced by the next request. Pierre-François has broken out of the groovy rhythm and suddenly stands next to me, abundantly perspiring and smiling. His body odor is particularly unpleasant for me. I literally can't stand the smell of him.

The funny lady comes back, and I hope to connect her with my dancer friend. But he comes closer to me. In that moment, I cannot avoid making a clear jump backward. A pure instinctive reaction. Female doesn't want to, understand? He must have noticed and understood that correctly. He was once so sensitive and registered things that other people don't even see, he once said. A gentleman who has just left the dance group joins us and tells about his life in Paris and how happy he is now to have moved back to the province. It is time for a sociable exchange in a good mood. The funny lady is now among us again and everyone praises their favorite dances. Pierre-François emphasizes that he prefers particularly the dashing, fast pieces. „And you?" The lady asks me slightly provocatively. „Are you moving at all?" „I guess I need a different kind of movement", is my answer. Without including the prana diet, I list the various exercises that I do every day. Suddenly the lady bursts into laughter and hides her face behind her hands. „Oh, you can't say that! You are so funny. You can't say that", she keeps repeating. I look questioningly at Pierre-François. He explains that the word somersault in French colloquialism means „to have sex".

Somersault is quite a normal word in the dictionary and the translation corresponds exactly to what I want to say, I argue. Yes, but everyone understands something else. This expression is no longer used so harmlessly in everyday language. And they all laugh loud and endlessly. Crap, I think, I really put my foot in it. I did not know that. They enjoy it so much and keep laughing. I am treating them unintentionally to a burst of laughter. Pierre-François and the funny lady enjoy chatting together, they burst with enthusiasm for the next dance. I push them away: „Of you go, the two of you", I shout and hope that they will intimately dance with each other.

I take advantage of the break to take a deep breath. I open the large sliding door and look upward to the night sky and the calm outside. I enjoy the stars, which always give me confidence and remind me of my home. When I come back in, the dancer is sitting in her chair: „Your friend is such an excellent dancer! You should definitely follow him at the next dance round! You and he go so well together", she feels compelled to add. Bad luck, my attempt was unsuccessful! Then she wants to pull me by the sleeve, when she joins the dance circle again. This is getting too much for me and I suddenly fight back. „That's enough now". She disappears with the other dancers. Pierre-François turns to me again, sweaty and laughing. Good for him that he is enjoying it. „It will soon be twelve o´clock and I would be happy, if we went home." I particularly appreciate the sleeping hours before midnight because they are of a particularly regenerating quality. Without any opposition we drive home immediately. He is cheerful and he enjoyed his evening.

So did I, I add, it was fun and interesting at the same time. Also from the ethnological point of view. I wasn't aware that people in this area would maintain the tradition so passionately.

„And the funny lady who really wanted to entice you to dance!" he emphasizes.

„Yes, she is an excellent dancer. She would be an excellent partner for you. I wish you a good night", I say rather abruptly, because I feel a strong need to finally be alone.

In response he jumps up to give me a good night kiss. His body odor makes me take a big step back again. Yes, yes, good night. I run up the stairs without turning back.

The housecat, the only one allowed in the house, the cat of the late partner Bella, is lying on my bed. She allegedly suffers from an incurable eye disease. Can't Pierre-François treat her? He is a healer. She has strange eyes and a strange look. I hardly dare to directly look at her. I am tired from the impressions of the day. I fall asleep right away, with the door ajar, so that the cat can go out, if she wants to. I find it particularly uncomfortable that his bedroom door is open all night. Just across from my room. I make a circle of protection around my room before I go to bed.


## THIRD DAY

As I wake up. Egyptian memories. On the way and visiting Blanche. The television evening.

Sleep is a little restless. What am I fighting against? I have no idea but there is a struggle for power. The cat is still where she was last night, always looking at me with the same strange eyes. I look at her angrily. Never in my life have I put on a grumpy facial expression for an animal. The cat has something compelling about her. She doesn't seem to be bothered by my staring at her, but makes a slight „meow" out of her sticky little mouth. The sound of her voice softens the hardness of my heart. I also find it particularly stupid to take out my displeasure on an animal. I caress her. I have a vague impression that she wants to drag me into something that I don't want to go to. „I should stop this magical thinking immediately. I am responsible for myself, my actions and my life", says my inner voice.

I go to the bathroom half awake. What I did not particularly notice before now catches my eye: The room is full of Egyptian statues: Isis busts are on every corner, even around the bathtub. Almost all of them are covered with dust and some with spider webs. Anubis, Osiris, Tutanchamon, Cleopatra, Acheput, Hator, the Egyptian cat, pharaohs stare at me with their piercing eyes framed by kohl.

Egypt, O beloved Egypt, where I enjoyed the greatest bliss after fleeing Atlantis, but also cried the most bitter tears of deception.

Vicky Wall was the first to point out my significant incarnations in Atlantis and later in Egypt. She did this in an impressive way, thanks to the color system that she received through channeling and that she called „Aura Soma®" It consists of over 100 two-colored bottles which reveal a precise color language. When I first drew the Aura Soma bottles, I chose the No. 18

yellow/purple, the „Egyptian Bottle". For a long time it was a beneficial oil for me as well as this precise color combination itself, as you can encounter it in a natural setting or in everyday life, for example, the Mimosa and the Bougainvillea tree in Sicily, which I have special memories of. But also, material combinations of these two complementary colors, or other constellations like my blood crystals under the microscope in the dark-field therapy. Later, in the course of my development, I resonated with another color combination.

I am standing naked in the bathroom; the eternal looks of Egyptians present stare at me. I spent a lot of time undressed in the Egyptian temples as a dancer during the sacred preparations! At that time, Pierre-François, as the Hierophant of the temple, ruled over the priestesses and holy dancers. Our destinies have crossed again and again. In other incarnations, he was also embodied as a sacred dancer. The atmosphere between priests and dancers was not only sacred. There was also much discord and betrayal, machinations, and sexual excesses. It was not uncommon for me to be involved in similar abuses of power in this era and in different hierarchies.

A strange story was the planned „short marriage" that I should have consumed with an older priest, whose incarnation was taken over by Pierre-François. I was very young, maybe 12 or 13 years old. He was a dominant, influential priest who needed the vitality of a young girl to regain his strength. I don't know why I rebelled at the time. Maybe I didn't like his body odor! My resistance caused great unrest, because on the one hand there were rivals who would have liked to take my privileged place, on the other hand priestesses who were responsible for ensuring that everything went smoothly according to the long tradition. The desired meeting between the old priest and me was not an accidental decision. Indeed, the guardians of the mysteries who could perceive the dancers' auras insisted on certain, subtle criteria in order to make their choice. I don't remember exactly how this situation ended, and frankly, I don't have the courage and the desire to go deeper into this story. However, a persistent image remains in my memory: that of the young priestess who runs away into the desert and is forcibly and forcefully returned to the basement of the temple shortly thereafter. It resembles a kind of harem, where the holy dancers were initiated, drilled, cared for, protected and looked after and kept away from external influences.

I would like to throw the entire gallery of dusty Egyptian statues out of the bathroom window. I take a deep breath and return to the current reality. In the garden I see the young man with schizophrenia again from behind. His aura is no longer so burdened, but he definitely needs help. I prayed for him, but decided not to do anything else. In this house I have to set clear boundaries because all residents have special needs and difficulties. The warm shower does me good.

I go down the stairs with heavy steps and speak loud and clear: „Good morning, Pierre-François". That way I want to announce that I am not available for any nonsense. My strict greeting meets with an icy „Bonjour". Well, I think the message has arrived. We can continue on a decent basis.

But the air is so dense, that I try to loosen it up a bit.

„Should I make you a coffee too?"

„Thank you, I've already had enough coffee."

„I know where we know each other from!" I throw cheerfully into the heavy atmosphere to loosen the mood, but above all to steer Pierre-François into a deeper discourse.

„Where from?" He is amazed.

„In ancient Egypt! We have had several incarnations together in Egypt." He turns a blank look at me.

„Don't you remember? No memory from Egypt?" I ask.

„No."

„But the bathroom is full of Egyptian statues!"

„I was dealing with Egypt, just as I have dealt with many other issues", he says in a dry tone, which definitely does not invite any conversation. I give up.

I drink my coffee in silence. I sit opposite my host at the table, where he arranges his coins carefully and systematically from morning to night. Then he tells me the plan for today: We drive to a friend, get in her car and go to a pretty little town called Honfleur. There we will have lunch in a good Chinese restaurant. Of course, I will not eat anything, but order a jasmine or a green tea. Afterwards we drive to a special market where collectors buy and sell coins and stamps. Blanche, the acquaintance, is a lovely woman and she is happy to meet me. Pierre-François intends to make a few bargains at the market.

The ice is broken. He is friendly. I like to take a ride and am happy to be away from the house and to discover the landscape. The trip to Blanche takes a couple of hours. I asked a short question about his youth that sparked a long, detailed answer. I gladly listen, even if I don't need so many details. It is about his previous sexual experiences, how easy and generous they were at that time. With the girlfriend and the girlfriend of the girlfriend and so on. Hopped into bed the same afternoon we met.

At some point it gets a bit too much of the same stuff for me! I went through the late 1960s and 1970s too, I say. I also tried a lot, out of curiosity and to find out what would be good for me. I deliberately gathered a lot of experiences, so as to find peace and not feel the need to catch up later. I think, you don't have to do the same thing over and over again. Different phases of life, different priorities. I basically like something new. That is evolution. The generosity of the so-called sexual revolution did not particularly appeal to me, even though I enjoyed a lot of freedom. It was not uncommon for me to feel dirty and lonely after intercourse. I often had the impression, that I had wasted something sacred on someone who was eager, but in a hurry to do his thing as if I wasn't really there. Most guys had little idea, although they thought they were a real gift to women.

I try to explain to Pierre-François why I don't see the so-called sexual revolution as solely positive. We were actually under pressure to behave like the others. Namely, never being able to say „no". I was picky, but I spared myself a lot from the start. It was not a real liberation, because the young people were unconscious and, above all, quite unprepared. Although I was well informed by my parents, a double standard seemed to be the order of the day, publicly and privately. On the outside, women were expected to behave in a prude and timid way, on the inside, they were supposed to act uninhibitedly, otherwise they were described as stuck and uptight. That was the benchmark for girls, of course. Men were allowed to act as they wanted and follow their instincts. They allegedly know how to do this through their special instinct, which they supposedly cannot control. What kind of masculinity is that? Such bottomless stupidity! In contrast, I discovered my feelings, my emotional and physical sensations and followed them. The attentiveness, the tenderness, the joy, the devotion, the beauty, the attention to detail, the consideration in dealing with each other as well as the care for the environment were so essential to me, but were often not valued or under-considered and most often just got lost. The former priestess in me lacked the ritualistic, the sacred encounter, the high-quality appreciation-power of devotion to the present moment and the holy act as well as its cosmic dimension. In the end, there was a feeling of emptiness despite a lot of movement. Like someone greedily and hastily swallowing a cheap, high-calorie meat burger with no real nutritional value and full of toxic additives. Shortly afterwards hunger plagues again, because the soul, the senses and the cells lack real nutrition, authentic enjoyment, satiety, and satisfaction. Was that the sexual revolution? Was that all?

We arrive at Blanche right away, so that the opposing views between Pierre-François and me do not have to confront each other. The uptight, top-heavy, strict old aunt against the eternal young-at-heart seducer, always ready, always funny. This is how I would visually compare our two positions!

Blanche lives in a beautiful house surrounded by a wonderful garden, that is well maintained and full of unusual plants and shrubs. As we step in the door, Pierre-François puts his arm around my shoulders and slightly pushes me forward. He introduces me to Blanche with the following words: „She is my partner.”

I feel dizzy. I raise my eyebrows! I think „What? I'm really in the wrong film!” But I can't find the English expression for it and remain speechless. Blanche hugs me kindly and kisses me firmly on both cheeks. Did she notice my discomfort? Did he feel my discomfort? He, who is so clairvoyant and sensitive, who supposedly sees and knows everything.

From now on I want him to clearly notice my reluctance, my avoidance-techniques and my refusal to take part in his game. Unfortunately, my maneuvers are covered by Blanche's bubbly hospitality and happiness. She wants to organize everything beautifully and perfectly for us and to receive us particularly generously. She reads every wish from Pierre-François's eyes. She is warmhearted, enthusiastic and has a golden heart. But she also seems naive to me. He gives her instructions and tasks to be performed. „Yes, yes, I´ll have everything ready, even if I have to get up at four in the morning”, she replies.

Blanche is versatile, she knows a lot about botany, painting, Buddhism and many other areas. She is very busy helping poor people, refugees and artists here and there. She participates in a wide variety of projects. I personally admire her openness, her spontaneity and her generosity. But I ask myself the following question: Has she a kind of dependency to him? What kind of relationship do they actually have with each other?

We visit Honfleur, a beautiful, well-kept town. Pierre-François now appears with his deep knowledge and shows us special places in the church and in the area as well as spots that have a special charisma. He fulfills this role with dignity and competence.

In the restaurant I sit across from him, so that I don't get his energies, chakra for chakra, completely. Blanche is happy to occupy this seat and sits directly opposite him. She talks non-stop, which gives me a break to think and watch.

It's good, that I'm dressed for the countryside with my hiking boots. Even if for this occasion I dressed a little more elegantly. I am wearing a fine dark blue top with laces and a chain made of beautifully cut blue sapphires. Once Pierre-François looks at me with desire and passion, but only briefly, until he meets my strict gaze. My „no-nonsense" look.

Blanche occupies the stage. I smile gently at their stories. Suddenly she realizes that he is not listening. He also admits that her stories bore him. That's why he switched off. She is briefly outraged, laughs, continues to talk and turns to me. I just give a short answer and she goes on. At some point he wants to go. She complains, that she has to pay for him again.

We drive a long way and finally reach the market with Blanche's car. Pierre-François is doing good business there. He is satisfied.

She follows him and carries everything for him. She keeps the overview. She enjoys supporting and advising him. She is the gray eminence behind this man.

He wants to go home. „No, not yet, come over to my place. I wanted to show and give you this and that and you have to pick up your car anyway." We spend a long time at Blanche's. She obviously enjoys his presence and doesn't want to let him go so easily. She shows us her garden, which is really extraordinary. Truly an oasis of light inhabited by etheric nature beings. Because she has gathered an exceptional knowledge of exotic vegetation, she grows rare plants. She is thrilled to share her enthusiasm, knowledge and skills, as well as the late summer splendor of her garden with us. I hold her in my heart. While Blanche and Pierre-François are talking I even see creatures of nature in a wilder part of the garden. They appear between the trees and the perennials. Beautiful! Suddenly, we, Blanche and I, are together and she confides in me that he is everything for her, everything she could ever wish in a man. „Great!" I start and want to add: „Go ahead, my dear, get on with it! I personally don't want anything from him!" Suddenly, he stands next to me. His unexpected appearance makes me silent. Blanche keeps bubbling on, anyway. At some point Pierre-François points his index finger in the direction of the wild part of the garden, where I had just seen natural beings. „It's nice there. Yes, there is good energy", he says, as we follow him there. „If you ever wanted to set up a bench, it would be a good place for it, the best one even." An unsolicited advice for Blanche. Apparently, he doesn't notice anything of the etheric life there. He vaguely feels that the energy is good. Everything is good and well. But where is this particularly sharp clairvoyance which he displays together with certain techniques in his brochures? Now, we're slowly parting and leaving.

I am now sitting in the car with my host on the way home. He doesn't speak very lovingly or respectfully about Blanche. She is too fat and babbles too much. Personally, I'm happy about Blanche's being so eager with conversation. I was allowed to be quiet and hold my energies together. After a pause, just as the car is standing at a traffic light, he leans in my direction and whispers in my ear: „I'm not used to waiting long for a woman." I can only be amazed at his macho arrogance and his pushiness. I am appalled. If we were outside, I would slap him in the face. Here in the narrow car and while driving I have practically no ability to react. „Pure arrogance." I laugh at him. At that moment, I can't pull myself together for a better reaction.

This is definitely not the way to seduce me. On the contrary. This behavior not only turns me off. But I develop an aversion for this man and his inappropriate behavior. I put on the heaviest chastity belt that has ever been made. The version with three locks (their keys being thrown into the sea). My dear, you definitely won't get me. I don't like your clumsy and tasteless approach. I expected a completely different behavior from such an intelligent, spiritual person, whose writings I do appreciate.

Everyone is a multidimensional being. Within our earthly existence there are different facets of maturation of the personality. Some parts can be highly developed, others more immature, because the development is varied and dependent on a life's tasks and lessons, as well as on the priorities of the soul and the specific circumstances of life. Above all, the versatile development is not necessarily synchronous among the different parts. I am considering how to deal with this new change. I hadn't expected that, and there was no sign that my host had altered in this way and what expectations he now projected on me.

He obviously feels lonely and is looking for a woman. Well, hasn't he learned yet that you need two for a relationship, or does he prefer a plastic doll? It certainly offers no resistance. Has the good man not yet found out, that the flower opens its calyx before the nectar is given? Does he not understand that the woman decides whether to open the door or not? Anyone who forces an opening or knocks down the door bears the deep violation of repentance that will haunt him for a long time. Because, crossing personal boundary and individual freewill carries a high price in the karmic context.

In the evening I am tense, irritable and in a bad mood. I would rather tell him to drive me straight away to the train station. But now there is no train until tomorrow morning.

Pierre-François turns on the television. Now a little distraction is just the right thing. We take a seat on two wide armchairs that stand side by side. I try to focus on the screen and dampen my mood. A little variety, pastime. I am usually not in favor of escaping or avoiding what should be dealt with and confronted. But right now, I just want to ignore this man. I pretend he's not here. With this my intention, I project myself into the screen and feel surrounded by the glamor of the event. It is a program where various dancing couples compete with each other.

The distraction is not entirely successful. I notice that he extends his left arm. And suddenly his hand is on the side of the armchair in my direction. First of all, I do not pay any attention. Then I look at it unobtrusively from the corner of my eye. Is he waiting for me to hold it tightly, to stroke it accidentally? I stare at it while searching for words. He uncomfortably pulls it back onto his armchair.

In addition to this uncomfortable situation, the television show is also unbearably stupid and superficial. At 9:15 p.m. I say goodbye for tonight. These days, the call to pre-midnight sleep is particularly early, I whisper sarcastically to myself as I walk up the stairs. The cat is lying on my bed. She doesn't even look at me when I enter the room.

## THE NIGHT

Nocturnal considerations.

During the whole night I have trouble sleeping, both falling asleep and staying asleep, which is extremely unusual for me, especially in my pranic state.

This strange situation is bothering me. Was I naive in my assumption that he is a serious person? Did I project an unfounded admiration on him? Am I completely mistaken? Did I get trapped somehow? I had never expected this kind of behavior and I am stunned by his trespassing my boundaries.

Generally and externally, Pierre-François is friendly. He takes me along everywhere. His children and acquaintances immediately accept me. But I don't want to be included in this „community". I am only a visitor here and I appreciate that everyone is so good-natured, but it is their world and not mine. I don't feel at home here. The unkempt, dirty, neglected old house makes me feel uncomfortable. It reminds me of my father's house: It was crammed with partly highly valuable things, but also with old beds, cupboards, blankets, wallpaper and so on. The smell of old, stale air builds up in my nostrils. I find the surroundings disgusting. The unkempt makes me sad: the lack of care, of mindfulness for the potential, the opportunities that are not attended to. My immediate surroundings are full of dust, I have little space to spread my things. I do not feel well. I am generally frugal and do not need much. But I find the dirt, the things that have been lying around for years, and the heavy energies that have accumulated rather depressing.

It's cold under the only blanket tonight.

The environment and the spirit of collecting, as well as the attitude and even the physical posture of Pierre-François remind me of my father. I assume, that collectors develop a similar level of care in dealing with their fine pieces: the methodic, the order, the enthusiasm, the dedication and the undivided attention among others. These skills develop within a framework that offers withdrawal and protection from reality. The focus is on the task. „You stop thinking", as my host admits. In this activity, the collector may find a space in which he can withdraw from the outside without having to deal with himself. There he finds an intact world where no confrontation or threat arises. This ideal world is inhabited by selected objects and established rules and values.

The parallels between my host and my father render this stay even more difficult to bear for me. In addition, my father's health has deteriorated to such an extent in recent weeks, that he could leave the earthly dimension at any time. Which makes him very present in my mind. I am expecting every day to receive a message from my sisters, that could tell me that he has passed away. Memories emerge, and I feel a deep gratitude for everything he has given me. And this, even if I sometimes rebelled against him or against what he wanted to force upon me.

Here, at Pierre-François', my discomfort is not only due to the house itself, but also to its remoteness. I like to be in the country, but when I can't come and go freely, I feel frustrated, locked up, dependent, like in a prison. I am used to enjoying my freedom of movement every day on public transport. I like to walk for hours. Tomorrow, Sunday, I shall walk to the village center four kilometers away, as there is no bus. Getting out will be beneficial. I fall asleep again with this thought.

A few hours later I wake up facing the pain of disappointment. I came here with the expectation to talk about spiritual issues. I am here to discover and learn new things, to regenerate myself in a spiritual atmosphere. I long for deep conversations, new considerations and a lot of wisdom in the exchange and in dealing with Pierre-François as author, healer, therapist and consultant.

What do I encounter? An everyday, superficial chat that avoids deeper topics in an instant. He seems to be completely tired of spiritual issues. He does not give the impression that he has somehow worked on himself or tried to integrate anything of his teachings. He presents himself as a mother's boy who earns the admiration of his mother, because he has succeeded in everything, unlike his sister. This sister has completely separated herself from the family. He has no contact with her and doesn't even know where she lives. He has no family members other than his mother. But his mother is proud that „he managed to be successful and well known". He has money, a house, children. And he copes very well with his complacency. If something is lacking, it is automatically up to the other person: his wife, sister, occasional work- or business-partners, also his clients, and so on.

But he is friendly and balanced in dealing with neighbors, with his children, with his friends. Towards me, he crosses more and more limits and gets slightly annoyed on a few occasions.

Where is the clairvoyant, the highly sensitive, the person who is aura-sighted and sees everything behind the facade? With me he sees absolutely nothing. I am simply a projection screen for his search for a woman.

He wrote about divination and various methods such as signs that can point to the future. Obviously, this knowledge did not serve him much with the two failed marriages. He doesn't want to know anything about my memories of Egypt. He is now retired! In my view, spirituality is not a profession, but a way of life and a way of being, a state of consciousness. This can be used professionally. But without a spiritual attitude there is no authentic passing on of spiritual knowledge and no personal coherence. You cannot say goodbye to it like to a job, a role, an object. Did he set up the function without being fully behind it? When he says that he had worked in so many professions, including as an actor, I now understand that in some situations he could only be acting.

It may be fascinating that someone is versatile and has a rich personality. But I'm less enthusiastic about his transformation: from a spiritual author to an older, neglected man, who absolutely wants to have a woman. His success with women in his youth give him an unshakable self-confidence. The swarm of women (if it was a swarm at all) is now over. Nowadays in general, and in my precise case, a woman insists that her feelings, her life situation and her own opinion are considered and included. A woman cannot simply be chosen like a piece of cattle. There must be mutual agreement, attraction and affection as well as a fundamental response and interest. Not only do I show no enthusiasm for his efforts, but rejection, rigor and demarcation. My reactions show avoidance rather than being accommodating or encouraging. Both, the tone and the content of my answers are becoming increasingly negative as well as clearly contradictory. I laugh a lot to ease the situation and because I find it ridiculous. How can I succumb to his endeavors? Have I projected positive qualities for this supposedly „spiritual man", that he really doesn't have? Does his acting talent reflect a manipulative fragmentation that wears a mask to hide the satisfaction of personal needs?

Pierre-François is not only in an outdated role-model full of unrealistic beliefs that are crumbling, but he also reveals himself as a narrow personality. It's about a macho who desperately wants a woman to maintain his hormonal level (as he was even informing me). It is about a lost little boy who is looking for a mother and, ultimately, a hardworking nurse who will look after him in his older years. However, these roles do not correspond either to my personality or to my future plans.

He told me that he was constantly in relationships with practically no transition from one partner to the next. As a result, he has enjoyed the support and inspiration of a woman without interruption, without the opportunity to practice being alone, just in the years when one is capable of learning. He has all my sympathy for this, because loneliness is all the more unbearable in old age. It is therefore understandable that he shows so much zeal to find a woman. However, escaping from being alone or even from loneliness is not his only motivation. But he makes the „natural" assumption, that when a man and a woman meet, a sexual relationship should arise. Especially if he likes her. Whether she likes him is of secondary importance. But not for me. I have denied this matter of course since my youth. I was always against this unwritten rule, which seems to be circulating even among women: she should feel flattered when he courts her. What a grace, that he cares about her! Even if he is clumsy or expresses his lust in a more or less appetizing way. He shows her his attention and inflates his ego. And should she feel honored, happy and thankful that he chooses her? What a sick game it is!

I am the queen sitting in the center of the labyrinth and watching how he moves towards me with care. I examine his deepest and most secret motives and explore the purity and generosity of his heart. I discover each of his natural inclinations and sense his ability to awaken. I appreciate every pursuit of fairness, self-respect and mindfulness. I pay attention to wisdom, balance, appreciation and dignity, both towards the self and towards the desired woman. I look forward to creativity and originality out??, the potential and spontaneity that arise from the heart. I am the queen in the center of the labyrinth, waiting for him, not only passively and receptively, but with an involved emotion and a wise determination. Do I decide to receive him, if he finds his way to me at all through the labyrinth? Is he suitable for me? Is there a deeper match between us? Is this encounter enriching for both of us? Is our approach to each other constructive and based on care and courtesy? Is the heart addressed to in both of us? Is there a magical attraction, the mystery of the alchemical attraction? Is there a concrete, practical basis for us to build upon? How does he progress in this labyrinth? How does he deal with failure, with frustration? Is he constant in his zeal? How authentic is his longing? Is it just a temporary thrill, a new achievement, or is his motivation entirely focused on fulfilling the soul?

I am the queen in the center of the maze, and I make the decision, whether we shall be a couple or not. What kind of being sis sitting behind the facade of the personality? That is what interests me.

However, he is not aware that he is being evaluated and he continues to trample on the old proven success and ego trip.

Uncouth and stubborn. Partly tasteless and pushy. No, that is not all right for me: Such a man does not attract me at all, and the circumstances are not suitable either. He doesn't perceive me as a person either, but rather as a woman who brings an end to his loneliness. Is there a reciprocity between us at all? Would I be satisfied with what he has to offer? Would I find fulfillment in this grubby, neglected house? Such considerations are alien to him and do not even have a small place in his mind. The immature person is self-centered. He has no place for the indispensable reciprocity.

I ask my driver, if he has learned lessons or gathered reflections from his failed marriages.

Basically, he didn't think much, but acted quickly and unscrupulously. And then, of course, there were the many other women ... Oh how interesting ... and I look out to the landscape as we drive. I ask geographic and historical questions as a distraction.

These are the thoughts that keep me awake during this troubled night. I play back the events and conversations of the day.

The puzzle for me is to understand how he wrote such good books, even though the whole thing seems foreign to him. He hasn't integrated anything. He does not live up to what he describes or recommends in his brochures, not even the diet. He does nothing and seems unable to deal with situations for which he is considered a specialist in certain circles. Pierre-François is completely unable to deal with the troubled young man whose symptoms are typical of a possession induced by drugs. The ex-spiritual teacher has provided valuable clues in his books. But in real life and in practice, he presents an ignorant and incompetent impression. He cannot have developed the knowledge himself. He must have the information from somewhere. The whole thing is a purely intellectual exercise and not wisdom that is practiced and lived. Even less a spiritual calling. That is the conclusion I draw from this closer acquaintance with him. It is a big disappointment for me, but I am happy to see through the illusion at this stage.

Nevertheless, I should finally go back to sleep. Of course, the cat is still at the end of the bed, watching me with half-open eyes. I try to ignore her, pretend that she's not there. Then I intend to gently remove her from the bed with my feet from under the covers. She stretches and scolds me softly. She then settles down on the other side of the bed, a little higher, so that she now comfortably lies at the back of my knee. I resign. I finally fall asleep with the liberating thought, that my host has planned something for himself tomorrow. I should then spend a large part of the day alone and free.

## FOURTH DAY

At last alone. Considerations. Over the roof. Father and son. The translation of my book. Bella's confession. Leading Bella into the light.

I hear Pierre-François get up early and leave the house shortly afterwards.

I doze for a while and decide to spend a nice day alone and to pursue my reading and other interests.

When I get up the sun is shining, and I intend to go for an extended walk today.

But first I spend rather a long time in the bathroom and with my spiritual and physical exercises. I enjoy drinking my morning tea and recovering from the restless night.

I feel great gratitude for the trust and generosity shown by Pierre-François, his family and friends. I am also grateful that the house is available to me. His daughter thinks, I'm „the right woman for him". He agrees and looks at me with sparkling eyes as he shares his daughter's enthusiasm about me. But I am not ready to „step into" this family. They have no idea of the interesting, self-determined life that I lead in my country of choice. They are neither interested in me personally nor ask about my life.

Strange how you can still want to „place" a woman today ... now in the 21st century in Europe. I also find it interesting how another woman takes on this role: in this case, the daughter for the father. Once, in a small town, I met a lady from a real estate office. She rented out rooms and small flats and thought that, as a French woman, I was the right tenant for the old man's apartment. I would be a good change from the nasty Russian woman, she claimed. Apartment and old man for rent: „two in one", so to speak! It's the hit of the year, isn't it? I don't know, if the Russian lady was a tenant first, but he had married her and had recently divorced her, because she insisted on inheriting the house, he told me. But I am not particularly fond of old men and I am not impressed by possessions. It was clear that I would keep this man at a healthy distance. And that was especially necessary for him, because he was the king of the trespassers of boundaries.

Actually, I should be happy that I immediately win people's trust and make a good impression. I appreciate the openness, but I never get involved in machinations. I can see the motivation behind the actions pretty quickly. Moreover, my intuition tells me, whether the terrain on which I am going is in line with my being or not as far as the inviting offer is concerned. For me the question is: Are my freedom and my individuality respected or not? Is the attractive offer a bait that leads to deprivation of my self-determination?

There was also this gentleman from the Middle East, very intelligent, highly educated, who had traveled the world, successful ... the dream-man, or almost. We met in a humble place where newcomers showed their art. We saw each other several times. This man was quite interesting, but sick in his psyche. My heart as a lover remained closed and I maintained a friendly but detached approach: I didn't open another door. He was wearing expensive clothes. I was not impressed, although I actually have a weakness for quality and beautiful fabrics. Then he picked me up in some luxury car and praised its qualities at length and how much it cost, until I started yawning. As long as a car is driving and I don't have to push it, the car is fine with me. He wanted to lend me money. No thank you, my freedom and independence are priceless. Financial dependency must be avoided, especially for women. Always keep an eye on your economic independence and rather eat potatoes all week than get hooked into a tricky situation, which can be very difficult to get out of. In addition, the fine gentleman lived in a broken-down marriage, where none of the partners wanted to divorce. He said, it would be ideal if I acted as a second woman. How do these men come up with such ideas in order to integrate me into their lives? Bullshit. I don't strive for anything like that. I have to live my own life, to fulfill my soul's mission, I want to savor my freedom and spend my money as I see fit, to spend my time as I like as well as make my own decisions. I am not available to fill empty spaces in other people's lives.

And now I have slipped into the role of the „right woman" for father. A premiere. Overnight I would become a wife, a mother-substitute for two grown children and grandmother for the grandchildren. Nice but not mine. Especially since I don't like the man himself, and even less every day. I am there for spiritual and intellectual reasons, because I am interested in his writings. I am here for a little inspiration, for a new orientation, for a fair and interesting exchange at eye level.

The monsieur does not see that in his blindness. No treatment, no lessons, no in-depth discussions, where I could pick up new knowledge and develop fascinating methods. No, he wants me by his side to fill the gap. As a writer, guru and extrovert man, he always had women who were at his disposal or whose dream was to get closer to the man on the stage. I have often had the opportunity to watch these women. They seem to expect a little charisma to flow over from the coveted man to themselves. Or they behave as if the privileged proximity would enhance their personality or lend them some other advantage. I always found these games degrading, especially within a spiritual or intellectual framework. I have also observed them in the political landscape.

I go out into the garden and laugh out loud! What kind of play is that? Is the lack of clarity in my project the reason for this distorted reality? Have I taken the decision too spontaneously? No, I decide, I'm in the right place here.

But now I'm enjoying this „day off" and the remaining days of my stay. Everything will be fine. My ex-teacher should have grasped my attitude by now. And I shall put him on the „teaching and knowledge" track, because that's the only thing that interests me here.

These are my considerations when I set off on a very isolated road towards the village. As a matter of fact, completely out of the way here. The autumn colors are magnificent, the chestnut trees magnificent in their majesty. The floor is covered with chestnuts, although the huge branches are still hampered by the thick green shells. Every now and then a car drives past. I walk for a long time until a queasy feeling takes over. Actually, I have no real desire to follow this lonely road. What would I do in the village anyway, it's Sunday? And nothing else is interesting there. So I decide to collect the beautiful, thick chestnuts in the hope that someone can process them. They are so thick, that in a short time I put together several kilograms which I can hardly carry home.

It is now early afternoon and I plan to explore the tiny village. For this I have to cross the group of houses first. The dogs, left alone at home by their owners, are all the wilder, for they take over the entire guarding responsibility of the property. Their barking is very loud and continuous. There is at least one animal per garden and sometimes up to three of them. They encourage one another in their eagerness and become more and more threatening. Then I approach a garden that has no actual fence. The dog could jump over the ropes that delimit the borders of the large garden at any time. I stop and feel within: „Is it a test according to the motto: confronting your fears?“ „No, it is a challenge to take a different path very realistically and reasonably“, I receive in response from my inner voice.

The other direction seems not only to be calmer at first, but much more attractive. The buildings have been extensively renovated. There are beautiful villas there. The gardens are well maintained. Yes, it seems like a better way. As if he were appearing out of a dream, a man crosses the path to disappear from one of the villas into the opposite one. All well, I tell myself, and keep walking. Suddenly three dogs appear from the left side. They are unattached, but they don't bark, making a rather unfriendly impression. I speak to them loudly and warmly. „I know you have your job to do, but I'm completely uninteresting and just want to walk past this way." I can hardly finish the sentence, when two more dogs appear on the right. I like animals and especially dogs. I can communicate quite well with them and I understand how they guard their area and so on. „Come back!" Says my inner voice. „Stop straining yourself. You don't have to prove yourself. Return to the house. You are trying to run away from this house. But there is no escape."

I decide to go back and spend time in the garden. It seems, as if I were alone in the whole place. Not even the young man with the psychosis is there. Everyone has flown off. To find out, I look at the house with my clairvoyant eyes. When I search the rooms with my X-ray vision, my eyes are drawn upwards by a blurred apparition above the house. There a figure floats almost transparently like a veil in front of the clouds. Even though I struggle to keep looking up because of the sunlight, my eyes stay focused on the shape. As if mesmerized, I try to make out the delicate cloudy shape. „Who is this? This person is not unknown to me" comes to my mind. „But yes", I suddenly say out loud. I am amazed to see that the woman is Bella. I recognize her from the photo that Pierre-François showed me. The longer I look at her features, the better I recognize her. And it seems, as if a very strange connection is unfolding between Bella and me. She knows me, because she has been hovering over the house in her astral body. I am now rather well acquainted with her through many of Pierre-François' stories. A gradually distorted smile appears on Bella′s lips. It starts frightening me. Then, without warning, her astral body dissolves over the house. In this instant, I feel very lonely with this experience. And above all unsettled. What does this astral phenomenon mean? Why is she so ambivalent? Is this an invitation to feel comfortable here, or a warning not to take root here and occupy her place next to my host? Since I don't have a good feeling, it can hardly be the bearer of positive news. I do not draw any premature conclusions and leave this experience for the time being. I trust that further insights and answers will be provided to me in good time.

Back in the house, I am writing a little in my new book. I am tired. When the world is so exciting and the night is so restless, dozing in the middle of the day is the best way to pass the time. Afterwards I do some reading and complete my subtle treatments. I exchange some messages.

Sometime in the late afternoon Pierre-François comes back. He has sold little. He immediately sits down at the table to arrange additional stamps and coins in his usual posture at the usual place. He seems happy that I spent the day alone without complaining or blaming him. Why should I? It was agreed from the start that he would spend Sunday at the market.

„The cat has completely adopted you", he says out of the blue. „She slept with you all night". I try not to make a big deal out of it. But he continues: „She is the cat of my last partner. She likes you." I think for myself: „Not just the daughter, but the cat and the partner from the afterlife, everyone thinks I'm suitable as a successor. But I don't want this honor." I deliberately change the subject.

Later that evening, his son comes over for supper. Exactly the same pattern continues to repeat itself. Pierre-François is the perfect son, and he is the complete opposite of his sister. I was told that she didn't manage to lead a decent life. It is the same with the current generation: Despite his young age, his son already owns property, has gathered professional success and even found „the right woman". The daughter Véronique, although much older than her brother, has only collected failures and problems until now. She has given birth to difficult children and still has not found a „real" man. She is a single parent and struggles with the material side of life. It saddens me to observe these stark contrasts and categories. Could it not be envisaged, that each child has a special task, occupies his or her place within the family and represents his or her own valuable and unique role? Isn't healing necessary for the whole family? The drastic division is a frozen pattern in this family. Moreover, the judgments between „successful" and „unsuccessful" divide it. And my „healer friend" has no insight into that pattern. I withdraw from this private matter. Nonetheless, I feel empathic towards the women who are painfully pushed into this scheme, but also for the men who, on the other hand, suffer from the pressure to succeed - even if their ego might benefit from it.

Father and son have a lively conversation about what's new in the environment and in the private sphere. It is nice to pursue their exchange energetically. Their affinity is heartwarming. Then the father makes a sexual joke about the son and his girlfriend and gives me a sly look. I find it rather out of place, especially since he adds a personal memory pertaining to the wife he was then married to. The son is embarrassed. Adult children feel a kind of shame towards their parents as far as sexuality is concerned, I have often noticed. It's not an issue for supper either, the son seems to think. And I find it tasteless of Pierre-François in front of his son and me to air out his sexual habits. In the course of my stay, this content reoccurs a few times in his conversations, especially in the presence of his son. Once he even describes an intimate situation between his mother and her lover. Does he want to draw attention to his relaxed attitude towards sex Does he want to pretend to be „cool"? He has already told me enough confidential information personally. His children don't particularly appreciate these topics. They are silent and look rather embarrassed. With a bored mine I look absently out of the window.

The son leaves us shortly after the tasteless joke.

Later, I talk to Pierre-François about my book which I am translating into French. On this occasion, I ask him to help me with language, more precisely with the spelling and the grammar. As I am not using French in my everyday life since the age of 18, I am no longer so proficient in the language, and some of my expressions are tinted by foreign languages. I wish we could tackle such a project during my stay. Pierre-François was a French teacher, so he has the best qualifications for this kind of work. After some corrections, he gets angry and vehemently criticizes my text. „It's about the language, not the content: that's the difference", I emphasize. „I am happy for any improvement and I am grateful for your qualified knowledge. But I take responsibility for the content." We are hardly several pages further, when he when he makes some strongly sarcastic remarks about .... „We cannot find a common denominator here either. Then we better leave this matter alone." I close the book, collect my sheets and pencils and wish him a restful night.

It is even better, if the evening together is short. I go up to my room.

Since it is so early, I cannot fall asleep. I lie deeply relaxed with my eyes open on my back. The cat lies along my right leg and starts meowing in a strange way. Delicately but emphatically. „What is it now?" I ask softly. The answer stares at me. It is as if I immediately could see through the roof and meet Bella's gaze. Yes, this is what is taking place. The cat purrs. The animal notices her former mistress, that is clear. It's a good thing I'm already lying down, otherwise I would fall over. I can't sink very deep anyway on the thin mattress. I am afraid and think: „Now the deceased partner is coming to settle the bill with me." Like this afternoon she smiles at me again with this indefinable expression, half friendly, half distorted.

„Bella, I promise I have no interest in your husband. I am here for spiritual reasons", I announce from the beginning.

„All the better", she says, which reinforces my uncanny feeling. „He is not yours and will never be yours", she continues. Now I'm really feeling uneasy.

„What can I do for you? We are not rivals. Can I help you in any way?"

„Yes, certainly. But leave him alone."

„He doesn't interest me at all. Not even from a spiritual perspective. I will be gone in a few days' time and it will be the end."

Bella doesn't seem to be particularly convinced.

Everything is getting to strange for me here. Not only do I fight the guy all the time, but on top of it, I have to justify myself towards his deceased friend. Thank God, my fiery temper comes to my rescue. No, no justification.

„Bella, you passed away three years ago, didn't you?"

„No idea.”

„But I do know! And I also know that you should continue further on your way and not hover over the house forever. Do you understand?”

„Yes, I understand, but I'm still in so much pain. And my lover wants to keep me with him.”

No, that's not true, I think. He's always had women since you left, or at least that's what he tells me. However, I keep this reflection to myself, because I do not want a dispute with his deceased ex.

„Bella, it's time for you to go into the light. You have to master your new tasks in the further dimensions, where you belong now. Shall I help you?”

„Yes, Yes. Please help me! Take the pain away from me.”

„Yes, dear, I shall. In addition, I will show you the way to the plane where you now belong. Do you agree?”

There is a silent moment. For some reason, she doesn't answer me. Then a question crops up in my mind and I ask her directly.

„Why doesn't your partner help you? Why doesn't he lead you into the light? That is one of his special skills. Or something he is particularly good at. He wrote a whole paper about it, didn't he?”

„Yes, but he can't.”

„What, he can't? I do not understand! I have already concluded that there are a few things he is unable to do, but he knows the procedure of escorting souls to the afterlife. He describes it in this excellent brochure. I have drawn inspiration from it myself on several occasions for my work."

„He can write, but can't do the work."

„Bella, what is this story? This is driving me crazy!" I'm annoyed. I am increasingly feeling tired, but I intend to accompany his former wife into the light, as she has been hanging over the house for so long.

„Yes, but I don't want you to send me away and then live with him. No, I'm staying here with him. I don't want him to take a wife again anyway. That is why everyone he has had after me is so weird. I am his only true love."

„Yes, you are. You are his dream woman forever and ever. Exactly, he told me that. But now you continue your life in the afterworld, and he remains here for the moment. At some point you will meet again and then you can fall in love again."

„No, I don't trust you. You want him as soon as I'm gone."

I am exhausted. She sucks off my strength, just as she deprives Pierre-François of his vitality. Now I have to tackle the situation and finish it neatly and quickly. I get up and disturb the cat at the same time. It does not matter. I am getting impatient and my dynamic self takes over the strategy.

„Bella, I raise your vibration to the next level and then you will see that you are feeling much better. Your pain will go away.

You will find your unique beauty again, just like on the picture your lover showed me. Let's do that together."

„Yes, gladly. But there is something else that is holding me back here. Something that makes my fate unbearable."

Bella starts crying. I had never seen a deceased crying so drastically. I envelop her with safety and love. I try to relieve her mental pain.

„Oh, you're so good to me", she says, relieved.

Everything is going so slowly. She is so firmly attached to the earthly plane, to her physical and emotional suffering, to her possessive love. I definitely have to put my impatience aside.

„Tell me, please, Bella what is your concern!"

„It is unforgivable, but I couldn't help it."

„What's so bad, please, tell me. Speaking out will bring you relief. After that, you can continue on the path of redemption with a light heart. I shall help you with it."

„No, it's so bad! You'll think I'm a hooker, a very bad woman!"

„I'm not here to judge. I am not a saint either. We are incarnated women, who have made mistakes on their life path. We strive to learn something from it to become wiser, more loving, more truthful, freer. Don't we?"

„But what I did is inexcusable. But I couldn't defend myself against this irresistible love. I was magically drawn into his orbit and couldn't resist at all. This relationship had to be, but at the same time it destroyed another life."

I now have an idea of what is captivating her in the earth's atmosphere.

„Your refusal to go further on your way is a bigger obstacle than what you accuse yourself of. I want you to give me the reason for you getting stuck telepathically. So you don't have tell it, if it's too hard for you."

„You are telepathic?" She is trying to save time.

„I am telepathic, empathetic and I don't know what!! And now we continue without judgment and without assuming anything about me. I have accompanied so many lives here and beyond, that I have long since stopped judging people. I try to understand and recognize patterns. No more. I know what it is anyway. Remember or say it, please! This step will be liberating for you instead of suppressing it."

The back and forth continues for a while, until I am completely annoyed and let go of the whole thing.

„Ok, you're not ready and that's your thing, your fate, your karma. Now I want to sleep. I'll be gone in a few days. And this story has nothing to do with me anymore. The schizophrenic, the daughter-victim, the macho bloke, the garden, the house, the cat, the girlfriend. You can live out all of your dramas forever. I didn't come here to heal or save this crazy family. Is that clear?"

„I understand. I'll tell you what's holding me back here on Earth." My impatient outburst shook Bella, and she is now willing to step forward.

„Then please do it! It's about cooperation. I can accompany you, but I cannot take over your karma or solve it for you."

„Yes, of course. I know all that. My sister and I shared the contents of the books with Pierre-François. We channeled the information for him."

„What!" I am startled. My blood seems to leave me, and I turn pale. At least that's my subjective impression. I see myself like a ghost resembling Bella. My Higher Instance is as ever present and sustains my organic reactions. My pulse beats excessively, but I can breathe deeply and can think ahead. My intellect works again. That makes sense: Pierre-François stopped writing three to four years ago, at the time when Bella fell ill and died.

„Yes, but Bella, that's not the reason why you're earthbound. It is an interpersonal matter. And it has to do with your sister. I ask you to share your concern with me, verbatim or telepathically", I add, hoping to bring her back into the context of our exchange.

„Hum. How do you do that telepathically?"

„Please keep it in mind, concentrate on the facts."

„I cannot. It is too terrible. I feel so guilty. I hate myself for it, but couldn't help it. It was, as if he was somehow forcing me to obey. I couldn't resist, his power over me was so great."

„I know." I relieve the pressure on Bella's astral body.

„That feels good. Now I can go through the pain, not just mine, but the pain I caused my sister. I stole my sister's husband ... Then he became my lover, the man of my life. And I am the woman of his life. That´s how it should be."

Bella is writhing with mental and physical pain. She condemns herself. She is in a dilemma. From her perspective, there seems to be no way out. And she has to pay for the happiness she experienced with Pierre-François.

I tell her this summarized analysis. She stops crying, looks at me with clear eyes.

„Please help me!"

„Indeed, I do! But I still have a short question: Did he practice love-magic?"

„Of course, and he made a lot of money with it. It's called reunification. His rituals have an irresistible effect", adds Bella.

The effect is not noticeable for me, I think to myself.

„And a lot of karmic bonds ... This activity is not recommended", I mean. „Thank you for this information, it is crucial for me, because there I can now start working and free you from these unbelievable bonds."

From the moment she confronts and accepts her story, it is possible to support her. I clarify her subtle bodies and open up the way for her. Of course, I am only an accompaniment: her cooperation and her consent are essential.

Completely unexpectedly, the process slows down when everything is going so well.

„What is holding you back now, Bella?" I want to know.

„But, tell me, you were his lover, weren't you? Admit it, tell the truth!"

Her beautiful ethereal charisma has become cloudy and distorted again. My powers are waning. I have to give her one last boost, otherwise all the trouble will have been in vain tonight.

„Yes, Bella! Naturally! But that was 5000 years ago, and since then it's finished, done, and over. I've been trying to make it clear to everyone for almost a week that I don't want anything from the man. Haven't you noticed that, when you hover and watch over the house all the time? And now, please continue. You are his true and only one." She moves on immediately. I accompany her in the name of her soul's liberation and in the name of Pierre-François' soul salvation.

I continue working energetically for a while. The mood is now calm. The stars shine through the roof window. I let the peace of the night carry me into the dimensions where I receive purification and regeneration in my sleep.

That is my intention when falling asleep. But the night will be entirely different.

# FIFTH DAY

Compliments and insect bites. Visit to Jeanne. The power places.

The fifth day starts with a surprising transformation.

My host is very friendly this morning and full of compliments for me. He is addressing himself to his daughter in my presence and describes me in the third person as a highly educated person with very specialized knowledge and deeper spiritual experiences. I have very special skills and I'm far too modest. It can be seen that I have worked very carefully on myself and that I have been polishing the inner diamond and so on.

All well and good, I think, but this unexpected chattering doesn't feel real. Why doesn't Pierre-François speak to me directly? I am present. What kind of theater is that? In the last few days, he mentioned, that I tend to underestimate my abilities, but generally his remarks are rather in a contemptuous tone related to my prude behavior. We are here on earth to enjoy life. It is about savoring the present moment to the fullest. Whether I was married at all was one of the questions that indicated that he considered me a stuck old spinster. I remained very vague and distant.

And I am even more distant this morning with this accumulation of artificial compliments. I am silent and put on an enigmatic smile. Above all, I wonder how long and how distorted he can keep up this flattery. He continues his line of compliments. I start to laugh inside and ask myself: „What does he want? To get me to bed this way? Why this turn?" My ego sees through the game and doesn't even feel inflated by it.

His talk is like a distraction, just when I want to tell him some unpleasant news. I won't mention Bella's treatment, but another event has taken place.

Because the last night was particularly restless. I have not experienced sleepless nights like this one for a long time. No, the insomnia is not due to brooding or the open bedroom door. Yes, it wasn't particularly warm for me. But that wasn't why I couldn't find sleep. Not even my encounter with Bella. The disruptive factor is a unique situation for me so far. Another premiere in this extraordinary stay.

I was kept awake by insect stings, I suspect fleas. And I hope it's nothing worse, like bed bugs or something like that. In fact, it's a whole new experience for me and I am not knowledgeable about insect stings. Although I often stay overnight at friends, acquaintances and strangers and in hotels or guest houses, I have never caught such a scratchy thing. I have never had lice, fleas or other insect bites except for mosquitoes. Practically all night from top to bottom, except on my face, I have been itching like crazy.

„What kind of bites are they? Do you often have this at home? Are the insects in the mattress? Or somewhere else in the room? The room is not particularly clean, it is very dusty. Did I wake up and activate any creature from its deep sleep? Are these bites contagious? Do you have a remedy for something like that?" I ask Pierre-François.

These are the questions that interrupt the wave of compliments rather abruptly. The tone changes, the vibration in the room tilts, his daughter leaves us, the facial features tense up. My gaze becomes inquiring and persists with a certain hardness, because I want to confront him and put an end to the nonsense. His gaze wanders and he avoids looking at me directly. The body language changes in a remarkable way, and I visualize the short section of a film in which a cockfight is shown. I am the smaller rooster, really fit and ready to fight. My counterpart is just as tall but broader in stature but not so fit and rather insecure, but his cockscomb is much more representative than mine. As in the film, the end of the fight, which can be really cruel and deadly under certain circumstances, is not shown. We have words for that. „Then you will take a memory from Normandy with you", he replies sarcastically. Once again I am speechless, for I was not expecting such a vile answer. Only then does my protagonist dare to look at me as if he had won a victory. No, I will not let it get me down. I say clearly and unequivocally: „I have never experienced anything like this, even though I travel a lot and to very different places..." He interrupts me: „It comes from the cat. These are the fleas of the cat and they are completely harmless to humans."

That is his diagnosis. I have often visited family members and friends who are pet owners. And never got insects bites in spite of their pets joining me in bed sometimes. Yes, I know that it is not hygienic, but it is so beneficial and soothing for humans and animals, both of whom get tanked up with magnetism. However, as I said, I have never been bitten by insects in this gross way. The cat is examined accordingly with the comb. Nothing is found in her fur. Then he reaches for the vacuum cleaner and quickly and casually cleans the main surface of the room without going into the corners or moving the furniture. Then he looks at me like a hero, holding the vacuum cleaner like the blessed weapon that has saved me. Actually, I could burst into laughter and roll onto this now clean floor! I don't want to get angry and keep the following thought to myself: „You could have done just that before I arrived, couldn't you?" Yes, he's is doing his best. I am otherwise so spoiled and know such wonderful people who have high standards. I am deeply grateful to everyone I know for their hospitality in such generous, caring and clean manner. It's a little different here. Basically, my host expected me to fall in love with him and slip into his bed straight away. Why bother to clean the small room and prepare the bed? But I insisted on actually getting the promised room for myself. „You will have a room for yourself", he said on the phone.

I kept washing the insect bites several times a day with organic apple cider vinegar. Vinegar is a wonderful fermented antibiotic agent with many special properties for internal and external health. It stinks a little. Everyone who knows me, appreciate that I have a fine nose and a predilection for essential oils and perfumes. But only Pierre-François has the honor to „experience me with vinegar smell". Maybe my new fragrance will keep him at a distance.

In the afternoon we drive to a colleague of Pierre-François, who is very ill. He visits her regularly to shop for her or to take her to the shops and the bank, depending on what her state of health permits. In fact, she is very sick and reminds me of people I cared for as a nurse. As I perceive her aura, I see that her life-force is very low and that her physical strength is hardly sufficient for the next few months.

Jeanne is in the final stages of a long terminal illness and can no longer be operated on. She is under morphine. She is on an infusion. She has decided to be looked after at home and receives a visit from the community nurse four times a week. The nurse is expected in about an hour, so Pierre-François and Jeanne want to shop quickly to be back in time. I stay in Jeanne's apartment, because there are only two seats in the car.

When they come back from the shop, Jeanne is completely exhausted. She can no longer maintain the good mood she was trying to put up before. She is in pain and demands this and that quickly and impatiently. I feel her discomfort. I am so sorry for her. To be honest, I wouldn't have expected her to go shopping and I was amazed that the two of them set off so briskly. Obviously, she overestimated her powers.

Jeanne is now back in bed, half-seated and slightly oblique. This posture is the most comfortable for her. She asks me, when we will see each other next time. The question makes me almost dizzy. Then she demands that I tell her a story. „Tell me about where we'll see each other again. You have special skills. I had some, too. Do tell me, how is it going to go on with me and when will we meet again?" At first, I am unable to make a sound. A part of her knows very well that her life expectation is rather short. That's why she was released. To die at home. Another aspect of her personality is avoiding to confront the situation.

I turn to my inner wisdom and ask for help. A very special story comes to my mind. A true story. I'm trying to push this proposal away. No, I can't tell her that! Impossible. Otherwise my head is empty. I only have this event in mind, which I clearly perceive with my third eye. I hear myself speak before I have made a conscious decision to do so. This report should be spoken out: It is dedicated to both Jeanne and Pierre-François. A personal experience, real life. Torn between the worlds, the thoughts the pictures and the words crowd in my perception.

Many years ago, before I consciously understood that I could see the dying during and after the transition, my old family doctor visited me. That afternoon I was sitting in the back of my shop. I tried to do the bookkeeping, and once again the results were not right. It was a plague for me every time. I was overwhelmed, annoyed, exhausted. I paused and tried to relax. I closed my eyes. Suddenly my childhood doctor was there. He knew four generations of our family. I remember how just and loving he was. He had a generous natural authority and was highly valued and respected by everyone. He liked me very much. He thought I was a special child and made all sorts of exceptions for me. He didn't vaccinate me then.

Although I haven't thought of him in decades, he now hovers between life and death in my mind's eye. I see him swaying between the two levels. But it is not yet time for him to go through the veil, he says. I call his name out loud and he looks at me with loving eyes before the scene gradually dissolves.

This story has had a long-lasting effect on me. This encounter deeply impressed me and raised many questions. I didn't know at that point that I was a „death walker". This term applies to people who can accompany souls on and over the threshold and travel back and forth to the otherworldly dimension, while they are still alive.

This part of the story is dedicated to Jeanne. I watch her with a caring look. Did she understand the message? If she wants, she can contact me when she is ready. We will meet again there, and I will help her on her way. She sinks into her bed peacefully. She looks like a child who is fascinated by a story without knowing exactly what it is about. My voice, my smile, my empathy, and the hope that such a story holds, lulls her into a deep relaxation.

Now back to the story, because it continues: Dr. B. is the only person I have experienced in this floating state between life and death. Everyone else who visited me went over pretty quickly and came to say goodbye. I wanted to clarify and understand this peculiarity. With this in mind, I contact my grandmother who is still alive.

„Is Dr. B. still alive?" I ask on the phone.

„Yes, of course. He no longer practices, because he is so old, but occasionally he pays visits to a few patients at home", she says.

„Do you have his address? I want to write him a letter."

There is a little unrest, a little stress in the background. My grandmother would be able to walk to his practice, but she doesn't remember his address right away.

So, Dr. B didn't go over. Maybe he can tell me what happened to him, so that I can understand his apparition in front of my third eye.

I am writing Dr. B. a letter describing my vision. I don't care whether he thinks I'm crazy. The interest is too important to me to pretend false courtesy. It's about this episode. I want to address this issue.

Shortly afterwards, I receive an answer from him. I recognize the noble handwriting of the prescriptions in the past. His writing style is new to me. I am amazed at these old-fashioned expressions: he expresses himself like my husband or a lover from the 19th century. So lovingly and caringly, but in a very formal way, he expresses the huge joy he felt as he received my letter. He has kept asking about me over the decades. My letter profoundly touched him. He was as impressed that I accompanied him in this particularly difficult phase. And above all, he expresses his inexhaustible love for me and how intensely connected he has felt with me since the beginning. The whole writing is expressed in a very elegant language, with a lot of respect for this wonderful woman that I am. I am moved to tears and I become this lady in the 19th century whom he loved so passionately. In those days, he was also my doctor. I was a young married woman, and he had fallen in love with me. The tragedy was, that despite his healing skills, he could not save me dying from my terminal illness. I died in his arms. I can't hold back my tears. As a child I had no idea of it: I simply enjoyed the attention and didn't really understand what he meant when he „thought I was a special child".

We are on the phone. In this conversation we talk like two adults at the beginning of the 21st century. He says that he almost died from the wrong treatment of young colleagues. Indeed, his soul spent several days floating between life and death. Then comes the moment when he looks back on his life, including the memory of his earlier years as a family doctor. At this very moment our perceptions intersect, and he appears to me in the back of my shop as I described it above. In addition, he tells me about the first acupuncture association in France, which he founded and managed. He meditated and he practiced Tai Chi. Besides, he always knew I had subtle skills. I do not mention the impression that his letter has made on me and how it beamed me into the 19th century. Somehow, we are both completely anchored in the current century now. We plan a meeting for the next time I visit my grandmother.

It is about a year later. Towards the end of the meal with my family at my grandmother's house, Dr. B. visits us and joins our cozy round. I would almost say that he hasn't aged since my childhood. Of course, this cannot be, because thirty-five years have passed. He also belongs to the kind of people who look almost ageless due to their awareness and lifestyle.

We are all very formal with each other. My family has maintained their high respect of him. The meeting is a little embarrassing for me: There is no trace of this special love bond from the other life. Our topic does not come up at all, because everyone talks about the past, about the changes, about their health. The magic of the vision is gone. The magic conjured up by our exchange of letters has evaporated. The return to the 20th century, the reality of our relationship, the palpable normality, I would even say the banality of our actual encounter, the dissolution and the untraceability of the „moment that has been there" rub against each other in a tender conflict that one cannot even name and can even less pronounce. A trace of melancholy, a hint of astonished expectations, an unfulfilled longing of the heart, a bittersweet aftertaste fill the empty space between our eyes. I briefly analyze the situation and prosaically think: „This love-story is now over.”

After a short time, Dr. B. would like to withdraw, and everyone says goodbye with a lot of gratitude. When it's my turn, he stands in front of me, hugs me very warmly: „I can hug you, I'm your old doctor”, he says to my astonishment. He whispers in my ear: „You were a special child. And you have become a special woman.” Then he gives me a very loud kiss, which seems to make everyone freeze in the silence of the farewell. Finally, my grandmother breaks the stillness with the same sentence that she used 45 years ago: „Dr. B. has a very special affection for Aurélienne.”

Maybe this love story isn't over yet ...

Since then I have never seen or heard from him. Since then, the emotional bond with our family doctor seems to have been erased. Or is it resting in the intermediate worlds, waiting for our next reunion full of memories?

Nevertheless, the two visions - his visit between the worlds and the remembrance induced by Dr. B.'s letter got triggered indirectly and unconsciously in me - keep their radiance and deep emotional power. But they are now self-contained. We have processed this bond. Since positive memories are connected with it, we are both free to either meet again in a future incarnation or not. If so, the emotional charge is not compulsory, but a relationship could develop on a more mature level, more mentally, intellectually, or even spiritually. For example, it would be possible as a complete fulfillment for it to unfold through mutual inspiration and complementary service to a common task. The affinity can continue to exist without having to fall in love.

Re-encountering people with whom we have had an intense relationship in previous incarnations is not uncommon these days. I have several clients who have met a man whom they believe to have known before. This feeling is shared with passion by both partners and is accompanied by astonishing agreement and reciprocity, mostly in a familiar environment such as at work, in a shop or in a place where the two partners go regularly. It is often a person whom they had not previously noticed or with whom they had a normal job or whatever for a while. I describe the constellation from a female perspective, because women are the ones who report it to me. Persons who otherwise follow strict moral principles fall head over heels in love with a colleague from work. Women who fundamentally put their family in the foreground, who would never be unfaithful or otherwise would never seduce a married man. Decent, responsible even humble women with husbands and children. Suddenly they only think of this coveted strange man. He is not that strange, because, as already mentioned, they meet often or even regularly in a professional context or within an everyday routine. Through the meeting, her whole life is turned upside down. Her connection to her internalized controlling and ordering aspects makes room for an overwhelming, unheard-of passion. She just wants to be with this new partner. Nevertheless, reasonable considerations are ingrained in her moral sense, and she doesn't just throw her 25 years of marriage overboard and leave her children. Maybe she lacks courage. She does, however, need firm confirmation that the man in question loves her as much as she does, even if he never seems to have time for her or if, of course, he goes home to his wife every evening after work. From another example: The boss, the company owner, who, although divorced and therefore free, has to be very careful because of his surroundings and his reputation. In short, there seems to be an inhibition that prevents a passionate encounter. Sometimes a single kiss happens, but it doesn't deepen the relationship. The unfulfilled longing, however, persists in the hope that the coveted man will eventually issue an invitation. This situation can drag on for several years without becoming more specific. On the one hand the female persons are convinced of the mutual love, on the other hand they come to me for a clarification. They want to know with for certain that he stands by them, for example, and whether he has the same feelings as they do for him, or that they will come together someday: When I ask practical questions about the situation of the current families and how exactly they would realistically manage children, husband and lover, they have no concrete idea. If no invitation from the coveted man ever happens, I suggest that they provoke the situation a little: „You can't wait forever, sometimes you have to hit the ball to get it rolling." And above all, a clear answer is needed: a no or a yes, which could clarify the entangled situation once and for all. In a fine, skillful way, of course, but even then, the women refuse to make a first step. Except in one case where the woman actually left her family (and later returned to her husband). In the whole constellation I see more of a strong projection mechanism. This has an important function: namely to add passion to a bland life that is usually dominated by duty and reason, and that is more than they have experienced in this life so far. As a result, this person discovers completely new aspects of her personality and gets closer to her essence through the activated emotional body. What my clairvoyance says about this is that this strong love is actually based on a former relationship with somebody in a previous incarnation. Therefore, a compelling mutual attraction is inevitable. In fact, they know each other on the soul level and have experienced marriage, loving relationships or a forbidden love. The emotions are overwhelming. But even if they can sweep you away, they are by no means proof that this relationship should be revived and nurtured and lived against all reasons in this life. In addition, this unexpected situation provides an impetus to make a mature decision about this conflict. By mature decision I mean a choice that lies beyond the fulfillment of the intense emotional longing and the satisfaction of the ego and the elementary drives. Most of the time, this magical encounter also offers an examination of the shadow side, which is accompanied by a diversity and intensification of the inner world of feelings. Indeed, the longing woman is called to a higher decision that transcends the balancing act between marriage, falling in love and loyalty.

The dilemma unbearably tugs on the strength and the basis of the old established beliefs for so long, that the answer must be beyond family habits and devotion to the loved one and the new life. From this a solution is born that is not black or white, but a result of the newly acquired connection to inner wisdom. The client discovers that it is not about deciding for one or the other, but for the SELF. In the best case, this distortion makes the person grow and encounter herself. Above all, however, she now discovers her wishes, her vision, which she then constantly implements in the existing family environment. Ultimately, she remains true to herself and independent of external events.

Occasionally, it may be that the woman who expects confirmation of her wishes, as she would do by a fortune teller, is disappointed with this answer. But I am not a fortune teller and can only give truthful answers for ethical reasons. Answers that help to understand the entangled situation and to understand the existing mechanisms. I am happy to provide assistance, clarity, new insights, compassion and recommendations, but the women have to make the decisions themselves.

Back to my host: I do not rule out that he is suffering from a similar deception from previous times. Nonetheless, this time is different between us. Moreover, I suspect very practical reasons why he does not want to continue to be single. Not only is loneliness difficult for him, but he alone is unable to find the drive to manage his life with the garden and everyday duties. And he's been looking for the right partner for a long time since Bella's passing away.

I now sit with Jeanne and as I tell the story I realize that the second part of the story is dedicated to Pierre-François. It's about ending an emotional bond. I look at him with piercing eyes. The whole thing seems embarrassing to him and he looks away towards Jeanne's bed. Right now, the nurse arrives, and we say goodbye to the ill lady.

We sit silently in the car. Then my driver talks about his answer to Jeanne's request, when she had asked him to give her a message a few months ago. He asked her what she wanted for Christmas. A nice idea, I say - although it is not obvious that she will still be with us until then. My long story is not commented on. He directs the conversation to an observation he made about Jeanne. He has felt a deep jealousy on Jeanne´s part towards me. He is able to perceive such things well. He notices things that other people don't feel or see. I emphasize that Jeanne is sick, even very seriously ill, and that such a feeling might be easily understandable. I am older than her and flaunt my health and strength. No, he replies, her jealousy relates to my closeness to him, because I am much closer to him than she ever was. I squint and swallow. What does this guy imagine? How can that be? I'm thinking so much that after a while I can only ask: „Are you serious?" In no time we are at the place of power.

I had asked to visit an energy place in the area. The intention of this visit is a spiritual and energetic exchange with him. Especially, because he is particularly knowledgeable, and the area is so rich in power places.

The sun is shining, the ground, too: I feel a strengthening, recharging and nourishing vibration from the earth. „This is the Yang place", explains Pierre-François. „Now I'm going to show you the yin spot. I have brought so many people to this place of power and shown them new paths over decades. Very special places that are hardly known", he adds.

Now he's in his element, I can see that. That's how I know him: in practice, a good teacher. He can clearly and specifically point out the essentials to the students. He is happy to pass on his knowledge, I am also very pleased. At last it is interesting for me. I express my gratitude. Then he comes too close to me and whispers in my ear: „It's a very nice day today." I instinctively take a step back. Immediately I become more serious and distant. If my cheerfulness and lightness are misinterpreted, I will clearly show my limits. Am I dealing with an inconsiderate person? „I am interested in what you are showing me now. That is one of the reasons for my stay here. I don't need more", is my really annoyed answer.

We then continue to another place and to a church by the sea, which is built on a power place. The landscape is beautiful, the mood between us is more subdued. This time my guide shows me the high-energy places, but also a place where the physical strength is clearly drained.

Back in the car we drive in silence for a while. Then he tells something about his sexuality. Just a short sentence. The idiot is back; he still hasn't understood that I'm not a solution for his marriage and sexual problems. What he is saying is a very special thing about his heroic behavior in bed. He inflates his battered masculinity by telling me intimate things. And it's always about his little, overrated body part. I just say „sick" and talk about something else as a distraction, like you do with children, so that they stop begging for sweets all the time.

He comes up with the motto „rather tell nonsense than sit quietly together". Actually, this attitude seems to be very common. I also used to feel under pressure to talk about something just for the sake of chattering. I have given it up now. The greatest thing is to find someone with whom I can sit comfortably and quietly for a while, so that both of us appreciate the silence without the urge to make noises with our mouths. To share stillness together and with confidence, to surrender to the moment without words.

Then Pierre-François asks me how I became pranic and how I maintain it. I explain to him in detail the methods I use, how they work and how I have adapted them to my personal needs over a year and a half. He listens and for once does not say a word. I'm amazed. „You don't make a beep. You know better otherwise, don't you?" So much the better if he doesn't say anything, because who doesn't know doesn't have anything to say. But yes, he only wants to point out that Jasmuheen died of it. I laugh out loud, because she is more alive than ever. I saw her on Skype a few weeks ago and read her last book. „Look at me: I'm healthy, fit, free, flexible and receptive to new things thanks to pranic food!" We close the topic, because we have nothing in common there either. He also thinks that Guantanamo has long been closed down. I can take him less and less seriously. I do not have a television and I do not read official media, but I make sure that I am well informed.

In the evening we sit together quietly, he is busy with his collection as usual and I occupy myself with the books that I have chosen from his library. Suddenly he verbally attacks me and talks negatively about feeding on Light and my condition. „Nothing works anymore, there is nothing at all, no interest in anything that could be fun. But man is on earth to be happy, to enjoy". The hedonistic lecture is then supplemented by a spiritual litany about love. „Only love counts and love opens the heart and heals everything. Man is evil in himself, as long as he has not discovered love..." For me also, the all-encompassing caring, the all-pervading love and light are the prerequisite and goal of existence. But I find his kind of opportunistic and superficial interpretation out of place.

Since I no longer take this person and his fits of expression seriously, I just stare at him and in no way get into a discussion with him. He's just frustrated. I am apparently the first woman who does not respond to his manipulations, his reputation, and his inflated self-confidence and fall prey to them. It is probably what he meant when he whispered in my ear at the beginning of my stay: „I am not used to waiting long for a woman!" In a simultaneously intrusive and overpowering tone. Hopefully it is the last time that he indulges in violating my boundaries. „Old habits die hard", the English claim. It's hard to let go of old, bad habits. Because women have become picky and insist on their independence and self-determination. For many who already live a fulfilling life, a relationship can only be entered into on the condition that it is an enrichment and that their quality of life is enhanced and, above all, that their freedom and independence are respected.

Basically, there should be an affinity between the partners. A woman is not „to have", because she is a woman. He did not even ask about my private life, nor about my professional career, my future plans, my obligations, my wishes, my interests. I live in a cosmopolitan city. What would I think of living in the country without public transport?

No, the good man only has a tunnel vision of his role as a desperate seducer. His behavior reveals the self-evident attitude that he is entitled to having a woman. Overconfidence obstructs everything that does not fit in his fairy tale. He simply ignores the fact that there is no reciprocity on my part. Men have behaved like that for a long time. This naive expectation, that a woman is flattered by his attention, has long been a thing of the past. Such an important man, a successful author who is valued as a well-known teacher in Normandy, a great landowner and so on. He is convinced that no woman could resist.

He would only need to look at me briefly, not even with his supposedly clairvoyant ability, to see that I am not this type of person. First of all, I am satisfied with who and what I am, and my freedom is my most valuable companion. Possession has never seduced me, neither roles nor prestige. I could fall in love with a pure soul with an uplifting striving, with an authentic and integral personality, with a warm, free heart. Above all, for me it is a matter of vibrations that flow between people. I perceive that on various levels. The resonance creates the connection, and it is the decisive factor that surpasses everything else, especially selfish desires and machinations. There is nothing to talk about. In addition, I have enough self-esteem and do not intend to forego my success, to leave my accomplishments behind, to give up my personal space and my freedom. I remain in my entirety and dedicate myself to my inner wedding with passion, and I celebrate this with a full heart and an alert mind. I remain true to my path.

Today, too, I end the day early. I concentrate on my meditations and my exercises.

# SIXTH DAY

Ambivalence of the situation. The collector. Disappointment. Reflections. In the collector's shop. Reorganizing family relationships. Favourite subject. Breach of trust. One more try. My anger. Véronique's session.

The sixth day is the penultimate of my stay with Pierre-François. I am proud that I have stayed and did not leave early, which I would have done a few years ago. I would have simply fled the overwhelming situation.

The strange thing about this kind of situation is the ambivalence: On the one hand everything looks nice and polite even caring from the outside, on the other hand there is a repeated disrespect and trespassing of the female boundaries and especially my personal and private realm. Everyone is nice to me, but the patriarch takes advantage of the situation, hoping to find his personal sexual fulfillment. How common is such behavior? How often do you encounter this quiet manipulation? How often does the patriarch outrageously exploit his superiority coupled with his good reputation? A few times he put pressure on me and made derogatory comments: I am not flexible, I am too rigid and not open at all. I am and remain stable. Above all, I am too valuable to act against my desire and self-respect. I can imagine that this kind of demarcation is not easy for some women, especially in the context of his ongoing attempts. Some might feel attracted to his land, to his reputation, and to his apparent self-confidence. Persistent violence is implicit in these stereotypes, even if it is belittled by both women and men. It's time to throw them overboard.

We don't have a program today. Oh, yes, we do! We drive to a friend of his, a collector, sometime in the afternoon. Right in the morning, the landlord is busy with his stamps and coins. The sky is overcast and it's cold outside. I am a little bored. The pace of this week is actually very slow for me. I have a quick grasp, and things have to go a little faster to be exciting and nourishing for me. Therefore I wonder how I'm going to spend the last few hours here.

Pierre-François is not in a good mood today. Actually, we no longer have any common topics for discussion or we quickly exhaust them. Properly walking in the village is hardly possible. I've had enough of the neglected garden. I ask him, if I can look at his specialized library. He brings me some books. A few hours later as he sees my zeal, he brings me more copies that are actually captivating to me regarding spiritual, esoteric and energetic matters. Each one of us withdraws into our own world, even though we are sitting at the same table. It is so. For both of us the stay turned out differently from what we had expected. The seducer has failed and the spiritual one is left empty-handed.

No, I do not go empty-handed: I bought some special energy devices from my host and learned a lot about distorted real-life images, about deception. I was able to meet the real character behind the external personality, the man behind the role of the author. A delusion has disappeared. A glare has dissolved. The poor reality behind the radiant appearance. I can still bridge this balancing act with compassion for the human being. The person who reluctantly assumes his true size and at the same time integrates his vulnerability and imperfection in his divinity. But it is more difficult for me to bridge the gap between the original author and the hormone-driven elderly gentleman, who cannot accept that I am not interested in his partner search, be it in the long or short term. It's a shame that this person is so easily controlled by his lower chakras. Too bad, that the insight is missing and that his respect for the female counterpart is nearly non-existent. What also strikes me as strange is that he does not live mindfully and has practically integrated nothing of the knowledge he deals with in his books. For example, he has no idea about living food or about essential, natural supplements. The matter is even more serious in the case of the young man: Although Pierre-François has written on such subjects, he appears to be completely incompetent in practice. Now I know from Bella where he got the information. Is it possible to have such specialized knowledge without integrating it, without wanting to live and implement it? This discrepancy is a mystery to me. Was it all just a matter of making money and gaining a reputation? Was that a role he played well? And now he's playing another one that's maybe more lucrative? At this point, I question myself and my striving to implement things that are meaningful and important to me. I am not even concerned with the perfection of the implementation. It's about the effort, integrity, conviction, knowledge and ability to live life on a day to day basis. Ultimately, it's about internal coherence. If this is completely missing, the credibility of the person is also lost for me.

Pierre-François' constant concern with his collection also makes any exchange rather difficult:  You could just say a few words...! But my conversation partner does not have enough concentration, attention or interest left for a lively conversation.

These abilities are literally swallowed up by the stamps and coins. In other words, he avoids any exchange: He defines himself within his small world, where he is still twenty and seduces women with his irresistible charisma. His gaze is directed to the past, to the time when he had to accept the disappointments that characterized his eternal search for the mother's attention. Again and again, he wanted to be such a good man: a perfect lover, so strong, so clever, so successful, so knowing, so quick in his reaction. His wish-fulfillment focuses alone on the loving mother or wife and is supposed to lure even more of the female admiration unto himself. Like a vampire who cannot accept refusal, because he is driven by his addiction.

The wives are the bad women who are to blame.

Out of the silence that prevails between us Pierre-François starts talking. „We are here to be happy, to enjoy ourselves and to have fun." That is his view. Mine sounds a bit more demanding, although we basically agree. The real happiness, which I prefer to call fulfillment, arises from harmony with the soul, and it is therefore present on all levels. Not in exaggerated excess, but in being and having what we are entitled to. Enough. No more and no less. A moderate fullness. Then, nothing is missing. Nothing to grab for fear of being alone or not getting enough of one or the other. In harmony with the soul, everything is there that is needed: meeting the right people, opportunities seem to emerge by chance, the means are there that are necessary for living and for carrying out projects. A higher alignment is achieved. No cheap hedonism, no quick saturation of the instincts, no „I have to" because „I want", but „Your will be done through me." From this perspective, fulfillment is not just a personal pursuit, but a duty towards creation - including humanity.

L´éternel féminin did appear in his life script: there she was, the perfect woman, for exactly seven years. Why did the woman, who symbolizes the fulfillment of his dream, die after this brief marital bliss? Had the power been sucked out of her system? Is that possible? It was an idyllic love story! Maybe, this perfect love is about energy robbing and a selfish power game? Maybe, it is time to put the images of this love fairy tale under the magnifying glass and pull them out of the subconscious into daylight?

I can ask such questions, but I cannot answer them generally. Everyone has to deal with them for him- or herself. Nevertheless, I do not want to have to accept anything that is offered to me as a matter of course, when it is truly not mine. It is precisely this „claim", and even more the blatant arrogance displayed by it that symbolizes outdated patriarchal patterns. The old role-playing game has had its days. Now we want to set up intelligent, appreciative, wise rules. Until we get that far, there may even be a break, so that both sides can reflect on how they want to meet again.

The break may even take some time. Because the persistent, rusted relationship- and thought patterns are firmly ingrained in the mind - and not only there! They will still cause frustration, disappointment, anger, grief and some broken hearts. These naive hearts that have been rocked into the rhythms of cheap love songs. Madness and deception are sung there: pure deception sown into the heart, and unrealistic expectations towards each other. A crime against humanity: The basic theme between man and woman is blown up like an irresponsible mirage, wrapped up like a poisonous bait in a sweet seduction. Instead of basic loyalty, respect, mindfulness, playful and enjoyable, complementary approaches, where you want to meet freely and trustingly at eye level. Yes, relationships in which freedom, loyalty and trust respectfully combine whether sexuality is involved or not. Time to shake things up, down to the bedclothes, until the restrictive, conflicting dependency roles… just drop out of bed.

It looks as if I am deeply engrossed in the books, but I am actually reflecting my own thoughts until it's time to get going.

I am visiting this city for the first time and I am looking forward to discovering something new. In the collector's shop, I am not introduced as the partner. I am not even noticed. It doesn't matter. I introduce myself with my first name and a handshake. I am here, and even if I never see this person in my life again and he wipes me out of his memory within 10 minutes, I still want to respectfully represent human existence, both mine and that of my counterpart. The conversation is irrelevant to me. I watch the energies around people, in the shop, in the café, and their interaction.

The meeting with the collector comes to an end after a short time. It is still early in the afternoon and Pierre-François wants to go home. I am horrified at the idea of driving straight home: I am not looking forward to spending the late afternoon and the whole evening reading, while Pierre-François is arranging his stamps. I ask, if there is an interesting place in the area where we could stop. No, he says, there is nothing worth visiting here. It is obvious, that my companion has lost all interest in me. Either I am the „partner", his dream projection, or I am not really existent.

Unexpectedly, a street sign appears that indicates the „devil's chair". „Turn right, please", I say impulsively „I would like to have a look at this location!" In the middle of the forest there are huge rocks surrounded by ponds and streams, a dreamlike place, but the vibration here seems strange and cruel to me. Pierre-François explains what the devil's chair is all about and that people were thrown from the highest rocks into the stormy river. Nature is enchanting, but humans have used this place for cruel rituals. „There are also telluric radiations and many underground water veins that have a rather negative impact on the frequency of the place", he adds. It is once again a pleasure to follow his geo-biological account. He knows the topic in detail from different angles. For me, this excursion is the highlight of the day. Now we're driving home.

Véronique, Pierre-François' daughter, is waiting for me. She would like to make an appointment for a session: „Would I answer some of her many questions?" She appreciates me. I would like to help her, because she suffered a lot in her childhood. Not only then, but also in the last few years in her marriage with the alcoholic husband. We agree on a time in the evening after she has put her son to bed. I immediately see in my mind that there will be some delay. „See you later!" I say in a cheerful tone. I look forward to this personal counseling with Véronique, who needs hope and encouragement. But I go straight up to the room where I start packing my things. I am happy to fly home tomorrow. I am overjoyed to be going back to my world! I am doing a few stretching exercises out of sheer joy and I am laughing softly to myself.

At some point I go back down. It is still early in the evening and Véronique has not yet managed to send to her three-year-old to bed. The little one unconsciously feels that his mother is up to something, wants to do something for herself, and this evening he is particularly enterprising and tireless. The grandson is as bulky as the grandpa. They don't get along very well, either. Secretly, I smile at the idea that Véronique and her father want to integrate me so eagerly as a family member: They couldn't wish for a more unsuitable mother-in-law or partner. Or, who knows, indeed the most appropriate one? Maybe it would be the best way to restore a little balance in this nest. I would teach the daughter to set up healthy boundaries, so that she can fend for herself against the assaulting ex-husband. I would show her all the subordination patterns she learned from her father as a child and teach her how to throw them overboard. I would literally put Grandpa back in his place and lock him up with the entire coin and stamp collection in the closet with the valuable dishes. I would teach junior that he can be a tyrant over ants and beetles and about nobody else (especially not about his mother, whom he should honour and respect). I would leave him alone in one of the grandfather's many fields until he is cured from his tantrums. That's how I would rearrange the family. But that would only be the beginning. For I would then order grandfather and grandson into the garden to clear up the mess. Then they could properly let off their respective stowed up energies ...

I am jerkily pulled out of these daydreams by „grandpa", as I now kindly call him (as long as I am not correspondently called Grandma)who is now taking a little break from his coins. There are women who rediscover their sexuality in the period of menopause, or discover it for the first time as a real pleasure then. And there are others who just give up their sexuality completely with the said menopause. Which would not be necessary at all, for these women only need „the right partner" to ... just steer them back on the sex track. Grandpa does not let go of his favourite topic.

„Since you retired from spirituality, you've only been talking about sexuality. All your consciousness has slipped into your second chakra. I activate my hormones when and with whom I want. Maybe this fixation is a sign of some aged brain decay?"

Pierre-François continues his treatise. The cherry on the cake is still to come. „But it is very different for men: even in old age, sexuality remains very active as in my case." I stare at him with a slight smile on my lips. „I'm not interested in that at all, understand?" I hear myself say as I flash back into my role as a nurse. At that time, I rarely witnessed aggressive behaviour with male patients. Only a few harmless occurrences took place. The nurse comes to the bed with the catheter-set and the patient makes a joke that is somewhat inadequate. In fact, it's about easing their own fears and embarrassment. It is important to remain purely professional and not to go into it at all.

Just like with Pierre-François now. I stare at him until it almost makes him uncomfortable.

I am getting impatient, because it is later than planned and Véronique is still not here. She lives next door and I can hear Junior putting up resistance and wanting to be told another story, or getting some chocolate or playing on her cell phone again. Then Véronique bursts in and apologizes, unfortunately it takes a little longer, but not so long ...

I understand her and I really appreciate Véronique. I want to give her something before I leave. Although I shall not read her aura, I will answer her questions and give her some hints on how she can deal better with herself. That is what she required, and I stick to it. An aura -reading might go too deep for her. However, she is not ready for it and has not asked for it. I am now looking into some of the spiritual books that my host has made available to me. In no case do I want to revive the virility issue again or open any door for it. I am in the book and he is in his coins as always. That is as much as we have as an exchange. Who knows what else he has simmering in terms of sexual issues?

I was expecting to encounter a deep spiritual source of wisdom, practical skills, experiences and suggestions. But nothing is there. His perceptions are obscure, he is useless, sees nothing. The landlord lacks the least judgment in the pragmatic sense as well as in the spiritual and psychic one. He bubbles away about superficial sayings that are common in the esoteric circles: He says he lives out his feminine side, because he cries when there is a sad love film on TV. A meaningless statement. A senseless cliché in my opinion. A show-off that has nothing to do with accepting his feminine side. I definitely don't cry about soaps. But there are many things that I can't bear indifferently: the gap between the poor and the rich, the humiliation of women, human trafficking, the exploitation of people, manipulation, injustice, lies and fraud, general repression and hypocrisy. I don't lose crocodile tears over them. In the worst case, I can't handle them properly and let myself be overwhelmed and suffer from insomnia. In the best case, I strive for awareness, information and sensible action. in order to contribute to a change. I certainly have no tears to lose about fictional stories.

Another wrong expectation I had about Pierre-François is a topic that I specifically discussed with him a few years ago. I had asked him to help me mentally in case I stepped into a dead end. I formally asked, if I could count on his help, whether he would help me in a spiritual crisis or if anything serious ever happened to me pertaining to my health. I would send him a text message. But it turns out that he doesn't read or send SMS! Why did he agree at the time and very clearly said: „Oui, oui, bien sûr!" Yes, yes, of course. Good thing the fraud is now emerging. Better find out in time. The unveiling is blatant. The dazzling puppet is hollow. Empty promise. In the moral sense „a breach of trust"!

In a few hours, hooray, I'll be sitting in Paris having a coffee on a café terrace and looking at the whole thing from a distance!

Véronique finally comes with a large writing pad and sits down at the table next to me. „Nice that it does work out", I say. „What is your first question?"

First, Pierre-François sits apart; and I think: „Congratulations! He respects his daughter and our private session, and he lets us work between women." A session is also a somewhat personal thing that requires distance from family and other close people.

Shortly thereafter, however, he takes a seat at the upper part of the table, which is usually occupied by the patriarch!

Véronique has prepared a whole list of questions. She is clear and intelligent, somewhat strict with itself. She speaks quickly and with an emphatic affect. Her emotional body is very stressed, and it would actually be urgent to clear it up and free Véronique from some heavy loads. However, I intend to stick to the agreement and only answer her questions, which means i.e. not to do any energy work. At some point my host sneaks into the conversation and emphasizes that Véronique finds me very pleasant, and that since the first day she has been claiming that I would be the right woman for him. „Il te faudrait une femme comme ça!" („You need a woman like her!") is the notorious saying, which he hammers home to me. Once more and as the very last chance he is again picking up this litany.

On the outside I remain polite and decent. Inwardly, however, I am turning into a hellcat. In a matter of seconds, I change into an uninhibited Lilith who hurls him through the room like an old rag doll, shouting at him until he is completely done. In my imagination. Lilith, the irrepressible, who does not suppress her frustration, but expresses it uninhibitedly. Lilith, who protects and defends her space and her rights. Lilith, who uses power directly and dares to contradict head-on.

At the same time, I remember scenes from a Canadian film in which an indigenous director thematized the internalized violence-fantasies of indigenous women. Of course, these women are no more violent than any others, but they have substantial reasons for wanting to fight back, which is little known in our latitudes. The heroine becomes a monster and takes revenge on her tormentors with oversized force. Of course, it is not a question of women imitating brutal male power. An eye for an eye never offers a solution. This film left an ambiguous impression on me. On the one hand, it is imperative to realistically recognize century-old humiliation, oppression and exploitation without hypocrisy. On the other hand, everything in the film is so exaggerated that limitless revenge becomes a parody. A parody that finds resonance in the deep injuries to women - not solely indigenous women. One day, weariness reaches the limits of what can be put up with and explodes like a volcano that has forever suppressed the inner magma and can no longer hold back the destructive innards at a given point. It is time to stop repression, time to address issues effectively with clear awareness, courageous justice and consistent behavior-changes as well as collective action. Back to the film that shocked me. Rather, my own reaction shocked me. I had to laugh out loud at this never before experienced bubbling wild female violence, which released a lot of aggressive potential in me and proved to be liberating. It was frankly not a „funny" laugh, but an emotional reaction vibrating with liberating resonance. I remember a sentence that troubled me as a child. „Girls have no aggression" was this incomprehensible claim. It even generated an existential question for me: „Am I not a girl then? How is that possible? What do I do with the anger in my guts?" Repress, confront, research, accept, understand, treat, in order to live it out creatively and to transform it through movement, self-assertion, self-determination and freedom. And to finally transcend it energetically and spiritually.

Now I would like to look into an obvious and subtle observation of the origin, the spread and the expression of violence in wars. Partly (and I emphasize „partly" because there are other reasons such as economic, political, power and manipulation purposes) wars arise because suppressed negative emotions accumulate as a dense cloud of aggression. It travels the earth to come down where there is resonance for it. These are areas where people are vulnerable because of poverty, frustration and other aggressive potential as well as crumbling political and social structures. Such places resonate with destructive energies. Nonetheless, the origin of the agglomeration of violence lies in completely different countries. Even in areas where negativity is suppressed and repressed to the point where one's own aggressions are not even perceived. Somewhere and at some point this accumulated energy has to be released and finds a way out. Since it is neither named nor accepted, it wanders energetically until it meets with a response as described. If we were to pay more attention to our own thoughts and register our repressed emotions, we would rather be able to reverse and live them healthy and creatively. Thus, the mass of banished and concentrated emotions, which desperately seeks its discharge in areas full of frustrations of this world, would be „processed" where it stems from. It should be added that the murderous brutality of the war serves as food for negative forces. Of course, there are also corrupt geopolitical interests in the game. I am not including them here, because I exclusively concentrate upon the energetic connections, which are less known.

Only in my imagination does my host lie like a doll torn into a thousand pieces. He's actually sitting here like a little boy trying to get mom's candy again. I look him straight into the eye and say with a serious expression and a deep tone that doesn't tolerate contradiction: „Now I'm talking to Véronique!"

She is a little bothered by the tension between her father and me. It's finally her turn. She has been waiting all week for it. Junior did his theater. And now this wrangling between her father and me. I now turn to my client with the secondary intention of excluding the father: „Now I would like to dedicate my time to you". She smiles. I am pleased to see that she shows self-respect and insists on having her own session, for she is now present and receptive.

She tends to demand a lot of herself. She exhibits strong ethical aspirations. I explain to her, that she can achieve even better and, above all, more reliable results by maintaining a more loving attitude towards herself and setting herself realistic goals. Suddenly she bursts into tears. All her self-loathing is now melting in my arms. She is going through a strong regression. She is relating about her childhood among an uncontrollable flow of tears. I lend her a hold with a light hug. Pierre-François also stands up and looks slightly distraught as his daughter sobs and keeps talking about mother and father. Some sentences, interrupted by her loud sobbing, are incomprehensible. The main thing now is her emotional discharge. Afterwards she will feel lighter. She looks at her father. I suggest, it may be a good idea, if he hugged her now. Both resist to the idea: „No, we don't do that. No hugs between father and daughter!" „Would you put a hug on a level with an incestuous gesture in this situation?" I ask. „We don't do that". No wonder that relationships between women and men are blurred in this family. Of course, I leave it at that. All the tension is gone. We end the session as well as this emotionally charged evening. We wish each other a good night. Véronique thanks me in a touching way. I try to bring a little humor into the situation and remind them to take good care of themselves.

## SEVENTH DAY

Early preparations. Wider connections. Rhetorical question. No arena. Divination. Wake up. We're leaving. Good-bye. In the train. The young man. On the plane. Boundary trespassing therapist. Hand on knee. At home.

As always, I get up early. But today I get up particularly early, because the local adventure is happily coming to an end. I want to make sure that I don't miss the plane. My few things are already packed. I do my exercises particularly extensively and thoroughly. Nevertheless, time seems to stand still. I finally go down the stairs to the living room.

Pierre-François has made coffee for me. He is more attentive this morning, as if he would like to leave a friendly impression. We clearly have found no common denominator. I have registered the manipulative, repeated trespassing of limits. I will deal with it later, with the clarity of the geographical and emotional distance. He gives me a jar of honey, since it is the only thing that I still consume occasionally.

I don't even feel like taking a last walk in the garden. Instead, I stand in front of the house and look up the roof. I cannot perceive

Bella's apparition. Neither can I sense her vibration or any feedback from her. This is a good sign: She has found her way into the light, her place on the other side. I at least contributed to something worthwhile during my stay then. Did Bella let go of her lover? Did she make peace with her sister? But that is no longer part of my job. It's cloudy outside. It doesn't make me sad, on the contrary, I am so happy to soon be able to regain my freedom and escape this libidinous man and his surroundings.

We're doing a little small talk to spend time avoiding the awkward silence. But the experiment doesn't go far. There is not much to say. Or should I be confrontational and provoke him head-on? Finally get some depth out of him? Show him his dependence on women? Reflect his tasteless behavior? Accuse his macho behavior? Question the split between the unconscious man and the spiritual author? Should I mention his plagiarism which lacks the sincerity of revealing the real authors? – No.

But the following considerations about this strange week also come to my mind: What is the point of this encounter? What is its meaning, not only for me personally, but generally, figuratively, symbolically? What are the seed patterns? How could I have handled it differently? What is my lesson in it? Are there any features in this story that can be found in interpersonal relationships, in society, in politics? What are the essence and the deeper intentions behind this interaction?

Every event that I am involved with has to do with me. This is a matter of course, which is often mentioned in the spiritual and therapeutic area but is not properly understood. But since everything is interconnected, personal history also relates directly to social, historical, sociological, religious and structural archetypes. After years of dealing with individual and personal aspects, I am fascinated today by the larger connections reaching up to planetary and cosmic dimensions. More and more amazing paradigms are unfolding. I can only encourage you to continue researching and tirelessly questioning the illusory world until it provides clear answers to see through it. This requires spiritual courage and above all the willingness to put your own blinders away.

Rhetorically, I ask Pierre-François the following question: „Which right allows a man to court a woman, regardless of her personal will and her decision-making power, her life situation, her reaction and her feedback?"

Then of course there is the topic of disappointment, the unmasking of the spiritual guru, who turns out to be a hormone-controlled elderly gentleman, who refuses to face the truth, namely that mutual interest is lacking. I fully understand his fear of growing old on his own or simply the need to share his life with a partner. Indeed, I can consider that one tries to send signals: „I would like you as a partner", or even better, to you have the courage to address the topic directly: „I can imagine us building an interesting community. What do you think of this? How are your feelings towards me?" But his recklessly disregarding the woman´s feedback and his persistent hooking are disgusting. Such behavior arises out of the mind that does not want to understand that „a no" means „no"; out of the head of a guy who says: „She says no, but she means yes" or „If I put pressure on her long enough, she will agree at some point". Such behavior can only arise from a sick head that thinks he has to „fight" for a woman at all costs.

Are we in an arena? No, we are dealing with resonance, with affinity, with agreement. The energy flows by itself or it doesn't. Non-reciprocity is always difficult to bear for the ego. I have empathy for this. Yes, it's painful to discover that someone doesn't want to play in the sandpit with me. A refusal, a rejection, regardless of the precise scope of an interpersonal relationship, is always difficult to bear, be it in the business world, the private world or within a friendship, a love affair, or in a hierarchy. It's basically the same topic. The affection is not returned, the project is one-sided. Respectful and voluntary interaction through energetic resonance: a natural agreement arises, which in turn promotes benevolent interaction. We care for each other and something unique arises from it: a work, play or love relationship. If the resonance is missing, it is impossible to force it. So calm down!

No deeper exchange here. I won't thank you for the week. My attempt to address our conflicting expectations fails. We remain silent. May silence contains truth and knowledge.

Unexpectedly, Pierre-François interrupts the stillness: „Somebody is expecting you at home?" His eyes stare at me like a jealous lover. Could it be, that he suddenly realizes that I am living my own life? His piercing gaze seems, for the first time, to see me as a real person. So far, I have been the projection screen of his desires or the revival of his youthful longings. Earlier, I was a woman to be conquered, who was supposed to confirm his irresistible masculinity. Now, my behaviour shatters this insurmountable self-conviction of the Casanova, who demands confirmation again and again. „I'm not used to waiting for a woman for so long", I say slowly. He knows, that I'm imitating his words.

The opening in the wall of the invincible castle of his male ego now shows a cruel crack and the embarrassing crumbling of its inviolability.

Time has run out now. The game is lost. Because it was never about time or waiting. It was about understanding that I am not a teammate. It is about grasping that there is no reciprocity. His gaze darkens and turns inward to allow a little insight. A slight confusion can be felt in the room. Maybe anger and disappointment on his part.

Then Pierre-François says with absolute conviction like an official announcement: „I will meet my life partner by Christmas at the latest."

My clairvoyant perception shows me, that he is dealing with an oracle that reveals this message to him. His intuition and his future projections have misled him several times. His fortune-telling rather reflects his wishful thinking. May he draw new hope from it. But, please, without me.

Divination hides the danger of projecting your own desires instead of presenting realistic options. A few years ago, it was possible to predict the future with a higher degree of probability than it is currently the case. „Why is that?" you will ask. Human behavior is less easily predictable, on the one hand, because possible opportunities are more diverse, on the other hand, because more people make use of their personal responsibility and free will to go their own way. This is good news: The self-determined attitude made possible by the awakening of the soul offers different paths of evolution. And they are more diverse than the restrictive channels of the new controlling world order. Nobody really knows, what the future of the earth will look like or how the time factor can be assessed. Personally, I limit myself to the tendencies anchored in the present, that are either strengthened, transformed, healed or given up, in order to shape the future in a fulfilling harmony with the client's soul. This allows an active, creative and creating work with responsibility and freedom. This is in contrast to a statement that may set a particular course of action or, as in Pierre-François' case, may include wishful thinking (or worse, a negative projection). Let us take our fate vigilantly, creatively and confidently in our own hands. His example is that of a tragic-comic personality who stares into his oracle more than he looks at the woman in front of him. Where is reality? In the cards, in the coffee grounds, in the head or in the human interaction embedded in the surrounding events and the self?

There is an important message for me as well as a confirmation of my careful statements and my careful steps into the future. I personally go ahead in alignment with my inner voice. This is the advice that I give to my clients. I also insist on reality-checks to determine what is really happening and how I am feeling. Disappointing insights may arise that may bring a new unexpected turn to the events. A mental pain may be felt, a waking awareness can mark a new path and may lead to the abandonment of the one that doesn't work out. I am a guidepost for Pierre-François, if he can accept me in this role. If not, he can see me as a prudish, non-eating aunt with silent lower chakras. It is up to him to decide and to his willingness to open up - namely, to question himself and to gain insights. I make the best of the situation, draw even more strength from within and, above all, I enjoy the beautiful, educational moments and laugh with all my heart at the weird ones!

I silently carry my suitcase to the main door of the house. Actually, this action is unnecessary in itself. Symbolically, however, I leave his world of deception avoiding honest and direct confrontation with the issues of his life. The next seduction is on its way. It takes place independently of the woman, since it basically has nothing to do with the woman herself. It is an eternal repetition, a self-fulfilling hollow game that should once again confirm its irresistibility.

Looking down from the stairs at the neglected garden I internally say goodbye, without thanking, to this place to where I shall never return.

It is much too early. Nevertheless, we are already leaving. Nothing is holding me back here. On the contrary, I have been in a tense starting position with all my muscles, ready for days. Pierre-François would like to show me something in the garden. Even if I have not got exactly what it is about, I hurry to deny his suggestion. I am afraid to arrive at the station too late. This excuse comes to my mind at the last moment. Because right now we don't want to write an exciting story anymore. Come on, it's time, I say impatiently, and I'm already in the car!

The way to the train station seems endless. The silence between Pierre-François and me is difficult. „You could cut it with a knife", was my mother's saying. „Even better with a saw", I would add. I almost shiver with joy at the thought that I'll soon be gone. Away from this uninteresting place. But above all, away from this man who cannot distinguish between his wishful thinking and reality, who is so obedient to his instincts that he keeps repeating himself trying to convince a woman who has no mutual feelings for him, from this man who is gazing back at his life with discontent. How sad!

The unrequited love that he has to accept now may lead him to reconsider a few things. The lack of communication, the inability to engage in a sensible exchange, the insights we could have gained together... But I am not a woman who grieves for a long time. Let us focus on the present and concrete situation. We spent enough hours together around the large wooden table. Too late for remorse!

As soon as we approach the train station, Marie is already waving happily. She came especially to bid me farewell. It touches me. But it is a little overdone. At least she will be happy. She is completely enthusiastic and hugs me and talks non-stop. She presses me tightly against her big soft breasts, as if I were a child. Her emotional farewell seems almost inappropriate to me, because we only met a few days ago. It was nice meeting her, but we are not „bosom friends".

Then I dread to say goodbye to Pierre-François. „Just quickly and ciao", I decide. I have no desire to thank him. Otherwise I would also have to say: „It was indeed very extraordinary to discover your real face behind the facade. I also found it outrageous to catch fleas here." Instead, we perform the usual ritual: right cheek, left cheek. But then he continues: once again on the right and once again on the left. Due to the surprise effect I am carried away and feel disgust for this undesirable closeness. Do you kiss four times in a row in this area? No, he simply pushed through his need to catch up and once again disrespected my boundaries. I stare straight at him. Very seriously and very angrily. Without saying a word and with decisive steps I walk to the platform. Without turning around

Since there are only two tracks, I find the right one straight away, but it is divided into a south and north sector, which I don't understand straight away. I notice that I am slightly disturbed by the farewell that took place in the shady station building. On the platform I am blinded by the sun and I feel disoriented for an instant. I am angry inside, that this person disregards my demarcation until the last moment. This game is a real exercise of power and a violation of the will of the woman in front of him.

No, that cannot be trivialized! I do not tolerate the argument, that is „He didn't do anything", „It's not that bad". I also do not accept any excuse that wants to see such behavior as affection for me or even an expression of love in it. Those who tolerate such persistent behavior will affirm and support further violation of personal limits of women, up to the act of raping.

Let us be clear and simple once and for all: love means respectful and careful treatment of fellow human beings, and, above all, mutual agreement. Besides, love doesn't cause pain. Pierre-

François' behavior is a self-centered and reckless violation of the integrity of his counterpart. He turns out to be a selfish person, who takes what he is not entitled to. In the material sense, this is called „stealing". From a moral point of view such a gesture does not seem to have a label. Or, I do not know any other words than manipulation, trespassing the limits, to rob what is not given voluntarily and heartily. What is stolen never benefits, because the thought forms always envelop the object, the event or the behavior. Taking without consent is an act against natural balance, because it is never associated with gratitude or joy.

Why force something, when you lose everything, namely respect, a true exchange, enrichment of reciprocity. There are so many areas that can fill the soul and heart.

Does this enforcement stem from the feeling that you are fundamentally not worthy of receiving what you are entitled to? Those, who can accept what is in resonance with their soul, are showered with gifts, so that all levels of the being are fulfilled, so that being free of „wanting" or grace can be attained. I mean it not in the least in the material sense, whereby the needs of everyday life are also taken care of, that is, no more and no less than is needed. However, the material is never a purpose and a meaning in and of itself. This is a huge misunderstanding, but it shapes this society and causes infinite misfortune and futile efforts.

Why fight or conquer? Battlefields and love are incompatible. Bringing both of these principles together is a pathological and unjustified mix up, basically intended to inflate the nullity of machism. With me it is completely fruitless, because I do not resonate with it. It may rather even provoke a backlash, so that everything is lost.

I am standing on the platform. I still have time until the train arrives. It is so warm that I try to stuff my sweater into the already overfilled suitcase. I am bending over the wide-open piece of luggage when I hear my name called several times, quickly and loudly.

Véronique rushes out of breath towards me. „I have been hurrying, I drove so fast on the motorway. It took longer at the employment office. I really wanted to thank you. You were so good to me. You have helped me a lot. You brought me luck. The counselor told me, that I had the right to financial support until the father pays the aliments for the children. I am so happy! At last, a new beginning for me!" she says quickly and choppily. Everything mixed-up. I am deeply touched. We hug each other warmly. I feel a heart-connection to her.

Maybe I came here for Véronique. I have clarified some false expectations, weighed new insights into karmic contexts and freed myself from them. And may my spiritual teacher and hospitable seducer compile some insights and happily enjoy his life!

None of us is mentioning the future. The time after this moment is not included. Not even: „Have a good journey", neither „We shall keep in touch" or „Let us know, when you've arrived home safely" or „We'll be on the phone" or „Maybe you will come back?" or „When shall we see each other again?" A visit without a future. Without consequences.

Now I'm happy to sit on the train alone. I'm looking forward to the big city. I am looking forward to flying home. I experience this moment as a liberation. I still have no idea how I want to relate further to Pierre-François.

First, I let the memories and the sensations take effect. Then I create a space to listen to my inner voice as well as to allow „coincidences" and signs. During this time I forget the whole thing and enjoy my freedom.

In Paris I order a coffee on a street terrace. For me an epitome of the big city, something superfluous, that you never need in the countryside. Not really in the city either. Don't all these people sitting on the terrace have no coffee at home? I finally treat myself to this symbolic cup of coffee. I can't stay long, because I have to reach my flight.

On the plane, I am not yet able to push the events of the week away from me. I'm in a free environment, but those last impressions keep me busy. The farewell-kisses haunt me with a very unpleasant aftertaste. I think of Marie, but I can in no way differentiate how she reacts to my behavior: Whether she welcomes my departure because she now has Pierre-François all to herself? Is she surprised by my ruthless way of leaving? Maybe, she didn't even register the details? I wish Marie all the best. May your idealization of your dream man not be abruptly disappointed.

I am extremely touched by Véronique's unexpected appearance on the platform. I have a real sympathy for her, and I am so glad that she gets support from the employment office. I am a little concerned about the responsibility she has taken pertaining to the young schizophrenic.

I caught a quick sight of him before getting into the car. His condition seemed worse, even more acute. Finally, I saw his confused, scared eyes. Nothing was done, not even by a spiritual healer or by someone who was supposed to free him from the possessing entities, as Pierre-François had wanted to do. I consider this a very worrying situation for everybody involved.

I shake myself like a dog to shake off those thoughts. I must realize that it is not my story and that I must leave the foreign karmic constellation back there. So much suffering that could be helped! Or should be prevented with a little reason, not even clairvoyance or psychiatric experience are required to guess how things might evolve. Hardly in a good manner.

On the flight, my thoughts wander to a colleague. A therapist who I value for her intelligence, integrity and reliability. She told me about an incident with a colleague who offered to take her on his team and rent her a practice room. They had arranged to meet in his practice to discuss the conditions. When the time came, and just as she was preparing to leave for the meeting place, she got a call from the colleague in question, who had meanwhile changed his mind and asked her to come to his private home.

So, Brigitte drives for her appointment to the therapist´s, whom she only knows professionally and superficially. Brigitte is an attractive, self-confident woman in her forties, she has travelled the world and she is very competent and respected in her specialty. She is also married and the mother of two children. Both therapists talk about room occupancy and costs, as is appropriate in this context. When they have discussed everything and Brigitte takes her last sip of tea, she notices a change in the behavior of her counterpart. Out of the blue he suggests that she undresses and that they both lie together so that he can feel their energies. Amazed and thinking that she misunderstood something, she smiles sheepishly and stammers: „What do you mean, I didn't understand?" The protagonist boldly repeats the instruction, which she firmly rejects. On this basis there is no possibility of cooperation at all. Terrified and trembling she leaves the cheeky man's living quarters. Together with a load of anger. How should such behavior be classified? Does he also behave like this with clients?

Isn't that an encroachment? An abuse of professional trust that is indispensable to every cooperation? Isn't it about transgressing personal space, about breaking the boundaries of the fundamental respect that every person is entitled to? My conclusion is that it is a matter of widespread power, pathological thinking and violent behavior, which must be ended by addressing it. But equally so by learning to defend oneself psychologically and physically, from childhood onward. Unfortunately, many are still ashamed, repress the event and withdraw into loneliness, self-directed hatred and a lack of self-worth. Understanding, listening, encouragement from fellow women, family and, last but not least, from the partner is urgently needed. Instead of humiliating jokes and trivialization. Because crimes such as rape and other violent attacks of this kind begin at first in the mind and in the preliminary stages of disrespect. The cowardice and the hypocrisy lie in the game of hide and seek, which of course cannot be „proven" and which, however, occurs on a daily basis. And this all in the 21st century. It is high time to make a huge leap in awareness concerning this theme, because there is no real progress in spite of technology and the digital world. Advanced in the material, backward in consciousness: this creates a distorted reality, like in these mirrors which sometimes make you seem big, sometimes small, sometimes thin, sometimes thick. We think we are much further than we really are. Let's start with a healthy base, and it needs to be cleaned thoroughly down to the old tricky corners.

These statements also apply to male persons whose inherent will and limits are also being violated, be it by other men or by women.

I sit on the train for an hour and then I'm at home in my own world. The gray, slightly rainy mood sets the stage for wandering thoughts that circle around my stay in Normandy. Involuntarily, they keep coming back to one of the several car-trips I did with Pierre-François. At first, I don't know exactly what it's all about. But gradually I get the impression that he liked to spend the driving time in intrusive conversations. I go on watching the familiar flat landscape, which is not so special, but which I enjoy every time I return from a journey. Suddenly I feel his hand on my left knee.

„What!" I say softly but dismayed. I had completely suppressed that! I don't remember when that happened, maybe on the third day of my stay? I can no longer classify it chronologically, because it was an eventful week! The idiot allows himself to do this without my consent! Obviously, I had not registered this gesture clearly. Now that it comes back to my mind, I'm horrified, but realize that I've become milder over the years.

I remember one incident when I was hitchhiking in Ireland at the age of 18. A rather insecure driver did just that, putting his hand on my knee without permission and uninvited, which made me very angry. Immediately I told him to stop and let me out of the car. Which he did on the spot. In no time I was standing completely disoriented in the middle of the countryside. No car driving past, the area completely remote. I blame myself for having reacted in a super impulsive manner again without thinking about the consequences. Now, I can't get away from the place. It looks like rain. And soon it will be night. The hopeless litany gets on my nerves. I pull myself together and walk in the direction that my intuition shows me. That was the right thing to do! Fend for myself immediately. Do not tolerate nonsense! Get out of the mess. That is the confirmation of my inner voice.

Pierre-François's context is completely different. I react in a different way from when I was 18, but still very efficiently. I wanted to slap him in the face, which is not a good idea when driving. We definitely don't want somersaults in the car on a busy road and cause an accident. And by that I don't mean „French somersaults". But rather I convey a message to him telepathically and energetically. I extract all the energy from my leg, so that it feels like a piece of dead matter: cold and lifeless. I can see the aura of my leg practically disappear. According to the motto: there is nothing under your hand. With a fright in his eyes he looks at me from the side. He doesn't know the trick. „Look out on the road and keep your hands to yourself when you drive", I say sarcastically. Sitting now on the train I could laugh out loud.

How happy I am to be back home!

## AFTER THE STAY IN THE NORMANDY

My father. Weighing up. Veronique. The radiant, multidimensional human. Bella's possessive love. Karmic connections. Beyond the illusory world. Let go. Dedication of the book to Véronique and other women.

I didn't hear anything else about my father for the rest of my stay in Normandy. Obviously, there is no improvement to be expected, but his basic condition is maintained by basic care. My sisters visit him regularly and give him all their love and mindfulness. I am infinitely grateful to them for that. Our father's dementia has been going on for years, and I wish him to be soon ultimately liberated from his suffering. I continue to support him with my energetic work.

My stay at Pierre-François´ requires thorough processing. I shall take a decision and position myself clearly in relation to this man. The geographical and emotional distance provide me with a welcome break which enables me to analyse the situation. To be honest, the decision has already been made.

However, I would like to discuss some things in depth. I am interested in the conclusions our friend has drawn from the whole exercise. Although I believe that I have seen through his relatively simple psychological inner landscape, it would be fair to confront him and take his perspective into account. Perhaps in a few months there will be a somewhat differentiated, insightful exchange. If that's not too much to ask...

I feel a certain obligation towards Véronique. Not only for her current situation, but also because of the serious experiences from her past, and not the least because she brings along a good potential as a healer. She has the qualities and talents of a therapist. Of course, only when she has processed her current difficulties and initiated the necessary trainings. There is still a long way to go, but the disposition is there. Before she fulfills her soul's task, she has to go through „the dark night of the soul" herself. She is a late developer. In her aura I can clearly distinguish that her soul has the potential to heal herself and other people through her transformative power. I would like to accompany her on her path, if she allows me to.

There is an event regarding Véronique that I left out during my stay in Normandy. On the very first day, her father told me that she was raped by her ex-husband in an entrance somewhere in a nearby town in the middle of the day. I immediately asked: Did you go to the police with her? Did you file a complaint? Does she have medical evidence? Has your daughter received psychological support and care? Pierre-François, in his usual

„easy going" stance, replied that „one" had already dealt with the situation. He claims that everyone here knows each other: „You don't want to cause any unnecessary problems", and further lame talk. I am appalled! There are laws nowadays, and it should be expected that police officers seriously deal with them and that appropriate support is offered by social services. An evasive, resigned answer regarding the financial poverty and general inadequacy of the local community structures is all that Pierre-François can come up with. I want to contest these statements straight away: there are so many dedicated people who work in these professions and who are tirelessly fighting for therapeutic and legal changes. Even if the desired or optimal goal is not achieved, every rape must be reported to the police ... And what about the witnesses in such towns, where everyone always knows everything? Didn't anyone help, were there any witness? Are they all shut up? I have trouble keeping my composure. But Pierre-François claims that Véronique is all right now. She is now living at his place.

At that point I still thought that my host was a capable healer and that he had given his own daughter the best of his mighty art. The „non-expert" was still hiding behind his convincing attitudes. Let's take the masks down and see what is behind them. At first, confusing things may appear: motivations, aspirations, psychological injuries, fears, misunderstandings and other factors that shape and control people. If we remove them one after the other in all clarity and with a lot of courage, the being will shine in its dazzling glory. The essence behind the personality, the essence behind the distorted. I don't know what makes Pierre-François behave the way he does. I do not yet understand the full extent of my encounter with this teacher – seducer – Egyptian priest.

I carry a pleasant message deep within me: The radiance of the essential being can already shine a light into the darkest corners of personal expression. Just look at you, how this current chalice of the divine shines through! Yes, here in this spontaneous selfie of the soul a light being in human form shines and searches for other sparkling, radiant beings! They have forgotten, ignored and ousted their light for eons, since darkness has settled upon earth... They have buried their luminosity deep in the benevolent bosom of Mother Earth. Sunk so deep that they no longer know where the treasure is! And they look far and wide to the next planet to dig and explore there, too. Stop! Wrong direction! Back, come back to the starting point, back to the radiant spark, deep in the earthly being. From this perspective, the miracles can be received in a multidimensional and human form in the here and now. The divine, incarnated in his ignorance, is awakening!

This is not blind mystical rhetoric, but an invitation to look for inner, quiet gifts. An invitation to a speleological exploration of the subterranean mental passages, saturated with sparkling crystals and other valuable diamonds still encased in the mother rock. You need to equip yourself with good shoes, a headlamp and a lot of courage. Yes, spiritual courage and above all: „Don't forget to turn on the headlamp! Please hold on, because there is a risk of slipping into the abyss!" No, no glorification of the abyss! No, enough of it in everyday life, in the media, in the art. Is it feasible not to sweep things under the carpet, but to tackle them and at the same time to turn the headlamp, the third eye of steady intent on the bright, blinding light? This is my aspiration, even if I involuntarily slip into the occasional delusion and the blender emerges as a deceptive ethereal spirit.

This is Véronique´s story and the reason why I don't want to let her down: her potential, her suffering and above all the trust that she has placed in me. Even if there are no future agreements, I feel connected to her for a long time and somehow committed to her.

I only have contact with Véronique through Pierre-François. After a few weeks, I call him and intend to exchange content, which may have matured and be enriched due to the temporal and spatial distance of insight and knowledge. But I come across the same well-known empty shell at the other end of the phone. That oui-oui-talk and lots of nice kisses. Non, merci! Not only is it difficult to pin down Pierre-François on a precise topic, but he immediately avoids it with an enigmatic „Why then? It's all good. No problem, non, non!" Obviously he is stuck in a general denial. He doesn't want to confront anything. Silence, do not question anything, continue as before? No, my dear. In this case, I completely forego our acquaintance.

I was probably transferred to the long list of inadequate women by the disappointed seducer: „Too thin, too silent, somersaults only on the yoga mat. In addition, stubborn, persistent, authoritarian and a real revolutionary". Thanks for the compliments. He still has his dream woman, on which he can project his ideals. The only woman apart from his mother who is good for something. After all.

Let's see, how Bella is getting on from her unearthly perspective. In fact, she found her way to her heavenly home. However, she is still concerned with guilt feelings towards her sister. When I visit her on the astral plane, where she is now, something amazing is revealed. I received insights about actions in this life, counterbalancing events of a previous incarnation. By that I mean this: Many years ago, the woman who was Bella's sister Flora, in this last life was the mistress of a famous count, whose wife died in despair and abandonment. Of course, Bella was the betrayed woman at the time and she died of an unclear energy-consuming illness. I saw how the former mistress of the castle grew weaker in that past incarnation, whereas her feelings of hate and revenge grew more and more in her next life. The dramatic thing is that she carries them along with herself into the hereafter. At the end of this incarnation, as the countess betrayed by her sister, she lost everything: honor, prestige, beauty and fame, her sisterly affection and the eternal love that the count had promised her. A long time later, a few decades in our era, she incarnated again as a woman with the ulterior motive of creating a balance. Bella is born as Flora's younger sister. Both are connected by a deep sibling love. So much, that they share a lot with each other, even after Flora´s wedding to Pierre-François. She is increasingly involved in the business of her brother-in-law, and her work is so valued that she moves with him to the Côte d'Azur, for one year and only for business reasons. The three of them agree that this arrangement should last only until the company is running properly. They expect the company to develop successfully in the South. If the finances are right, they will return to Normandy and live happily ever after. In fact, everything is going according to plan at the beginning: good mood is prevailing, cooperation is bearing fruit and the company is growing rapidly. The success is amazing, the income rises beyond hope. As agreed, sister and husband regularly journey home to Normandy to visit the sister and wife. In the lives of all three young people all wishes come true. The couple and the sister/sister in law are completely satisfied.

And so is the character of the human being. that he always has more desires: that is in his nature as creator. Perhaps also in its greedy aspect? In fact, desire urges Pierre-François and Bella to get closer. Initially, both have inhibitions and take care of the wife and sister. Especially Bella is suffering. She has resisted Pierre-François' approaches for a long time, until he persistently presented his hedonistic philosophy: we are here to be happy. Her story takes many turns until the inner urge and the outer time pressure does the rest. Soon they will have to go back to Normandy. In six months or even earlier, because the business is running so successfully and has established itself so well in the South that it could actually be run from home. But it is wonderful here, maybe we shall stay a little longer ... Bella's last moral resistance is cleared by Pierre-François´ love magic.

„Bella, can you say that for sure? That is a very serious statement! Are you sure that he used his knowledge for manipulative and selfish purposes to take you as his beloved?" I demand with a certain severity. „For your part, you brought your karmic burdens along, they also have their weight. You shouldn't neglect that either."

„He told me about it, and he implemented it immediately. I didn't believe it, but then I felt the irresistible attraction, even when I was still resisting and doubting, whether I really wanted to be his lover.

„What were your observations?" Is my question.

„I no longer had my own will. As if I had no power in my mind. Compassion for my sister also disappeared. Before that, I took great care of her well-being. Then I became more and more indifferent to her. I didn't think about the consequences of my actions, especially the pain she would feel, if she discovered the change in the relationship between her husband and me. I only thought of myself, of us, of our undiminished happiness generated by an unexpected material abundance."

„How long did this phase drag on?" I ask Bella before the powers slowly wane. This type of communication costs a lot of energy for both sides.

„In the end, we stayed on the Côte d´Azur for two years until we finally returned to Normandy. It was then clear to everyone that we were an inseparable couple. And then it was hell: first with my sister and the divorce between the two, and then, when calm seemed to come back, I was gradually visited by uncanny symptoms that finished me within three years. The price of this love was so high, that I will never let go of Pierre-François. It is my one and all forever and ever. He belongs to me and to me alone. I am his only true love."

Bella's presence disappears. I can hardly hear her last words. After such a communication I am easily confused and dazed and feel a typical head pressure. I must move, air the room, breathe deeply, in another word: ground myself.

A romantic love story, do you think, that extends beyond space and time? No, the motives are selfish and are based on revenge and property claims. A need for balance and unconscious retribution from Bella's previous incarnation as well as manipulative attachment resulting from Pierre-François' magic tricks box. Even if I try and downsize the matter, I don't want to trivialize it.

On the contrary, any act that violates ethical rules and impairs the free will of another person has karmic consequences. These consequences call for compensation and not – I emphasize – not for punishment. The counterweight corresponds to the fundamental quality of nature, which always seeks to restore energy balance, be it in the case of events or in the physical body.

And if you think Bella died of an incurable disease, because she became her brother-in-law's lover, you might consider another reason. The cause of her illness is related to her guilt feelings and her gnawing remorse for her sister. Pierre-François' magical influence and the resulting partner reunification has left her in a quandary where neither of the two options - to fall for him and to hurt her sister – is acceptable? for her moral sense. That is the way the hopeless situation appears to her. She gradually succumbed to the fateful tugging dilemma by developing her lymphatic disease.

Have I spoilt your enjoyment of love stories? Am I the mystic who demystifies your tale and reveals unexpected complications? Of course, there is such a thing as love, true love, that connects souls to one another in freedom. As opposed to bonds that protagonists cannot escape through many incarnations. Pure love is experienced in a completely different way: It does not hold anyone in deadlocked roles. Above all, it does not demand revenge.

Bella and Pierre-François´ relationship represents still a different aspect. Her compulsive bond will not release her. In his present lifetime and in the next karmic encounters he will be unable to let go of the setbacks of his action and Bella's possessive effects. Also, in this incarnation he is no longer able to establish a relationship with a new partner.

This knowledge grips my heart. With the help of my higher instance I would have the ability to release both involved in this heavy karma. I wonder, if I should phone Pierre-François and let him know of my plans. Simultaneously, I would work with Bella energetically and telepathically. However, the consent of both is essential. The outcome of such a liberation of the soul would release both partners. After this work the relationship would no longer be difficult, even if the stored memories would still lend a familiar „taste" to the connection, because nothing gets forgotten. Nevertheless, both souls would have the opportunity to have an unencumbered couple relationship. They would also have the opportunity or the choice to experience any other human variation of a complementary, creative and fulfilling connection.

All good deeds and benevolent intentions remain stored in the deepest layers of the soul and of the cells. That is what characterizes positive karma. Love bears the seeds of intimacy and affection that characterize loving relationships.

The bond between Bella and Pierre-François has serious consequences for both of them equally, as well as for the sister and divorced wife, and also for the coming generations. Of course, it would be easier for me to work energetically with Bella in the afterlife than on the telephone with Pierre-François. When I try to set up a practical and ethical model, I suddenly feel sick and I receive the image of a female contorted face that screams at me. And at the same time, I notice a man who smiles at me ironically and maliciously. I immediately recognize Pierre-François, which rather shocks me. Immediately afterwards I know exactly who the woman is, who doesn't want any help! Without a doubt, the two are none other than „my friends" from Normandy! I immediately understand the message: my interference is definitely not appreciated. I must keep away from it and let Pierre-François and Bella progress at their own pace. It is none of my business now, I should refrain from getting involved with their karmic path. Bella´s progressing into the light is already a positive asset. No more is suitable at the moment. On the contrary, it would have fatal consequences.

Now, I should let go of it myself, thank this family from the bottom of my heart, envelop them with all-encompassing love and send them the best wishes for their next karmic encounters - of course telepathically.

It is not easy for me to say goodbye to Véronique.

With gratitude, I dedicate this book to Véronique and to all women who are hurt by humiliations, injuries and other abuses of power: May they all give birth to their new selves through the healing power of transformation and attain liberation by creating a new, compassionate world, characterized by deep insights into worldly and cosmic relationships.

On October 9th, 2018, my beloved father leaves the earthly plane and thus concludes his incarnation in this life. Gratitude is the only truth that sparkles from the cooling ashes.

The warping of time hides miracles of light and lets the future ahead shine in a compressed and uncompromising development of consciousness.

# Literary reference

Aurélienne Dauguet

**LIGHT-NUTRITION**

**MY NEW LIFE AS A BREATHARIAN**



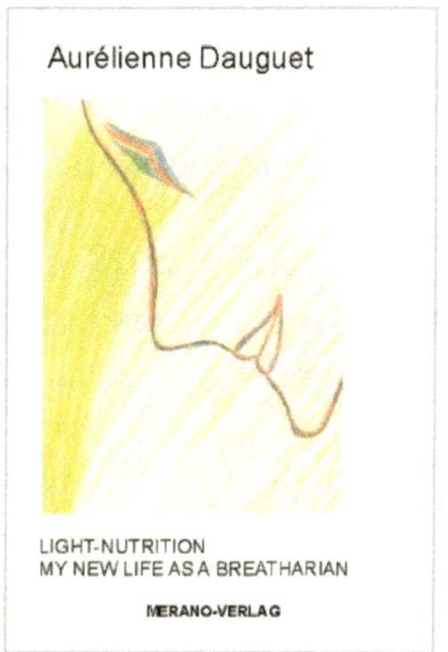


This is the report of the author's light food process. She entrusts us with how she managed to switch from „normal" food to photon food. We accompany her with light food during the first year of her new pranic life.

This description is authentic, down to earth, clear and simple.

The purpose of her contribution is to make understanding and intellectual access to light food easier and more realistic.

Nobody should be encouraged to do this. This process is a purely internal process, a call from the soul. There is nothing to prove here and no one to convince.

For the author, the decision to feed on prana was one of the most important in her life, with the freedom to stop or continue light-nutrition at any time.

English edition:

**LIGHT-NUTRITION**

**MY NEW LIFE AS A BREATHARIAN**

ISBN: 978-3-944700-18-2 (paperback)

ISBN: 978-3-944700-28-1 (e-book)

French edition:

**NOURRITURE LUMINEUSE**

**MA NOUVELLE VIE AVEC LE PRANISME**

ISBN: 978-3-944700-07-6 (paperback)

ISBN: 978-3-944700-67-0 (e-book)

German edition:

**Mein neues Leben mit der Lichtnahrung**

ISBN 978-3-96240-554-0 (paperback)

ISBN 978-3-96240-555-7 (hardcover)

ISBN 978-3-96240-556-4 (e-book)

Aurélienne Dauguet

**Reiseführer zu deinen kosmischen Energien - Aura Entdeckung**

**(Guide to your cosmic energies) (Aura discovery)**

**Only published in German language.**

ISBN 978-3-944700-02-1 (paperback)

ISBN 978-3-944700-12-0 (e-book)

Everything that is alive has an aura.

The energies subtle. Perceiving the energy wavelengths is part of the natural talent of all living beings. This ability opened a fresh, new look at everyday life and wide horizons.

The book „Guide to Your Cosmic Energies - Aura Discovery" takes the reader on a journey of discovery into the different levels and dimensions of the human aura.

It contains both theoretical treatises on the different layers of the aura, such as the etheric, the emotional or the mental body, as well as practical exercises for the correct handling of the aura.

Ultimately, the book becomes a guide for the reader to himself.

Aurélienne Dauguet

**AURATHERAPIE**

**für ÄRZTE, THERAPEUTEN und interessierte LAIEN**

**(AURATHERAPY)**
**(for DOCTORS, THERAPISTS and interested laymen)**

Only published in German language.

ISBN 978-3-96051-055-0 (paperback)

ISBN 978-3-96051-056-7 (hardcover)

ISBN 978-3-96051-057-4 (e-book)



This book consists of two parts:

The focus of the textbook is on the theoretical background, on the aura and the different subtle layers. Energetic approaches to the subtle anatomy are considered. The various aura pathologies and their harmonization are discussed in detail. The clairvoyant access to past and future, incarnational experiences, prophylactic aura care and aura surgery are presented and integrated into the therapeutic framework.

The practice book contains practice-oriented exercises that train the subtle perceptions of the therapist, and techniques that maintain, protect, clarify, harmonize and treat the aura and its dimensions. It also contains field reports that underpin the theory and implementation of aura therapy, as well as inventions by the author.

# About the author

Aurélienne Dauguet (born in Paris in 1953) has had a pronounced subtle perception since her youth.

Initially working as a nurse (plus psychiatric nursing), she is now a lecturer at the Paracelsus schools in Germany and Switzerland for aura therapy, radionics without device, the dying process from a holistic perspective, spiritual healing etc.

The current teaching offer is available from the Paracelsus schools.

Further training: lithotherapy, aura work, aromatherapy, flower and gem essence, radiesthesia, subtle radionics (without device), „Radionic Practitioner" according to the „British Radionic Association" and with David Tansley, Aura Soma ® training with Vicky Wall. Aurélienne Dauguet was one of the first Aura Soma teachers.

The teaching and seminar activities on the topic of aura take place throughout Europe.

For about 30 years she has been offering reading and cleaning of the aura, advice, individual sessions, individual lessons and remote support in German, English and French, both in her own rooms and by telephone.

If interested, see contact details.

Contact:
Aurélienne Dauguet
Please only SMS on 0049 1759421791
E-mail: aureliennedauguet@gmx.de